Chris Welford & Jackie Sykes

Staying

in Business

A practical guide to sanity, success and satisfaction at work

sane.works

Staying Sane in Business
A practical guide to sanity, success and satisfaction at work
© Chris Welford & Jackie Sykes
ISBN 978-0-993201-90-5

Published in 2015 by sane.works
sane.works is an imprint of Sixth Sense Publishing.
Reprinted in 2017

Permissions

Acknowledgements

We are indebted to everyone who has provided the inspiration, support and constructive criticism that has made this book possible. In particular we would like to thank Robin Hobbes and Karen Blumenfeld for what they have taught us; Dr Michael Brown for his excellent contribution to Part 2 of the book; Sarah Williams of The Book Consultancy for her knowledge and coaching regarding book production; Jon Hassett, Ross Collier and the team at Global River for their help on the sane.works website; photographers Neil Barrett, Altrincham, and Hills & Saunders, Maidenhead; all of the people who have read, commented on and endorsed this work and our friends and families who have had the kindness and patience to stick with us whilst the book has gradually come to life.

Lastly we really want to acknowledge each other for practising what we preach by providing the mutual appreciation and support that enables us to stay sane in business.

Contents

Chris Welford

People are a source of continual fascination to me – their motives, their drive, how they think and how they behave. This has been true for as long as I can remember! Whether we are alone, in a family or team, as a part of a large organisation or as citizens of a state, I wonder what makes us all tick; what lies beneath who we appear to be on the surface and what governs the way we act.

Over many years, working in HR, as a management consultant, a business psychologist, coach and registered psychotherapist, I have built up a picture of what seems to matter time and time again: what makes those who are exceptional truly different; how corporate culture excites and motivates us and how it sometimes turns us off and how extraordinary leaders do their jobs. Sometimes it feels to me like I am on a lifelong quest to understand the complexities of human nature. Maybe that in itself is a good thing?

My career has taken me all over the world and I have been lucky enough to have worked with hundreds of senior managers as an assessor, coach and team facilitator. I'm trusted by leading organisations to offer insight, advice and support and my clients tell me this is always delivered in a warm, inclusive and engaging way. You can read more of my thoughts in *Coaching at Work*, *HR Magazine*, *HR Review*, *Personnel Today*, *Management-Issues.com* and *Edge* magazine.

Jackie Sykes

When I was a toddler I started to ask the question 'Why?' and my curiosity has never subsided. As a teenager I made up my mind to be a psychologist and the enthusiasm I feel for my vocation is undiminished. From the beginning it was the world of organisations that caught my attention and in particular the way we behave in business. Over the last twenty years it has been a privilege to work with so many interesting and varied companies across the UK and internationally and in such a diverse range of sectors and functions. No day is the same and every client I work with is a source of endless fascination to me.

I'm a pragmatist; a driven and positive person who turns ideas into action. I believe that business psychology, neurolinguistic programming and psychotherapy have so much to offer the world. Whether I'm carrying out an in-depth assessment, working one to one with someone on his or her personal development, facilitating a team build or running a workshop, I keep coming back to the idea of potential. It's my belief that we are all capable of so much more: individually and collectively. My goal is to help to enable my clients to be the best possible versions of themselves they can be. We all deserve sanity, success and satisfaction at work and sometimes we need a little support along the way so that we feel like an effective and efficient cog in the right wheel of life!

This has been an incredible journey for me, starting off in psychometric research and test publication, moving through HR consultancy and line management and now co-directing my own assessment, development, coaching and therapy business. I am looking forward to the next chapter as a new author and hope our observations add value to others in the business of work!

'An excellent book that is full of useful advice on dealing with the inevitable pressures of coping with others, understanding their own strengths and how to develop them. Particularly useful are the practical suggestions and exercises on techniques to help the reader cope better with their own reactions, thoughts and behaviours when under pressure whether that be with the job itself or dealing with others and working as part of a team.'

Peter Saville, Founder, 10X Psychology

'A grounded and ground-breaking book that provides an easy to apply guide to managing all those stressful dramas work brings us. Taking a clearly put together, easy to grasp, practical social psychological perspective, this is *the* manual for sane work.'

Robin Hobbes, Founder, Elan Training & Development, former Chair of British TA Association and current European TA Ethical Advisor

'Focused, useful and a very interesting read. Great insight into what is a complex subject area but accessible and importantly relevant to anyone in business large or small – excellent.'

Julia Warren, Group HR Director, Trinity Mirror

'This is a very easy-to-read and practical book informed both by academic research and consulting assignments. I can imagine all sorts of work-stressed people gaining real insight and good advice from each of the chapters.'

Professor Adrian Furnham, Professor of Psychology, University College London

'Jackie and Chris have cleverly blended their own substantial and highly effective direct experience as coaches with leading research and empirical data to create this thoughtful and exceptionally accessible book and guide. *Staying Sane in Business* will undoubtedly be valued by a wide range of individuals across the private, public and not-for-profit sectors who want to understand more about their working environments, achieve more personally and for their teams, and understand practically how to go about doing so. It should be read by experienced leaders, those just setting out in the world of work, and everyone interested in how to make their contributions at work as valuable and successful as possible.'

Matthew Reed, CEO, The Children's Society

'This book provides an excellent toolkit with which to navigate the anxieties and pitfalls of contemporary organisational life – and remain sane in the process. It offers eminently practical advice on how to understand why we behave as we do and how we can go about changing our behaviours when they are counter-productive in a work context. Most importantly, it provides very useful and accessible advice as to how we can grow as human beings.'

Dr Sheila Keegan, Founder, Campbell Keegan Ltd

'It is rare to find such an excellent combination of textbook business psychology clearly explained, coupled with an extensive range of practical tools and techniques, that can be used by almost every personality type in almost all work and personal relationship situations. Above all, it is very accessible, which means that I can and do keep turning to it repeatedly, quickly enabling me to establish or re-establish my own control or understanding of the situations I find myself in.'

Stephen Mann, Chief Executive, Police Mutual

'*Staying Sane in Business* is an attempt by two psychologists/management consultants to provide practical tips on how to manage the pressure of business, relationships at work, and balancing work and life. Their remedies are very practical and easy to understand and should help in the stress-ridden world of work.'

Sir Cary Cooper, Professor of Organisational Psychology and Health, Manchester Business School

'This useful book draws on a wide range of psychological ideas and gets them across in a practical way. The authors provide "top tips" that condense many of the core ideas to provide simple and memorable guidance.'

Ivan Robertson, Emeritus Professor of Organisational Psychology at Manchester Business School and Founder Director of Robertson Cooper Ltd

'I enjoyed reading the book and was impressed by the range and depth of ideas and resources that are gathered here. By using the focus on one person (albeit a fictional Martha) and realising what can be done by offering and accepting help it is a useful tool for people in business. Staying sane is a lifetime occupation and this book will aid anyone who reads it to take some steps along the way.'

Bishop Tim Thornton, Diocese of Truro

Foreword

This book has been written for anyone who faces the rough and tumble of work, with all the messy and complex web of relationships that this entails. Whether you are employed or have your own business, it is from your colleagues, clients, stakeholders and suppliers that you draw energy and inspiration, while, at other times, it can be those very same people who make you feel as though you are going insane!

Work can be an inspiration – or a weight on our shoulders. (Photo by CW)

Staying Sane?

It has been accepted for thousands of years that the key to wellbeing is *mens sana in corpore sano* – a healthy mind in a healthy body. This book addresses the first. Here we look at the mental processes that lead to happiness, resilience and productivity. We don't specifically address the physical side of the equation in detail – diet, exercise, sleep, relaxation and nutrition – but that's not to say we don't believe looking after your body is of any less importance.

You can look at sanity in lots of different ways. It may be that you think of it as an absence of mental illness, or possibly you are drawn to the slightly wider idea of sanity being freedom from dis-*ease*: freedom from the suffering, alienation and unhappiness that can be part of life.

Either way, we don't think the definition of sanity belongs solely to psychiatrists, psychotherapists or psychologists. For us, sanity is simply being happy, fulfilled and productive. These are states we can all aspire to. Unfortunately, the world of work has a nasty habit of bending us out of shape.

Definition of a Business

Our definition of a business is a broad one. It's an organisation or economic system in which goods and services are exchanged for one another or for money. We don't make any particular distinction between businesses that are privately owned, not-for-profit or state-owned. Large organisations tend to be more complex than small ones but exactly the same patterns of human behaviour play out wherever you are. So, whether you are working in a multi-national or a corner shop, we hope that you will find something between these covers that is useful, relevant and interesting to you.

The Reader

This book is written for people who:

- Usually find business books a bit boring and who have picked up this book in the hope that it won't be dense, dull or full of waffle!
- Are starved of time and have started more books than they have finished.
- Would like us to get to the point and not stray off it.
- Are only interested in psychology and psychotherapy to the extent that either is useful in everyday life.
- Want outcomes, not aspirations.

The Authors

This book is written by two individuals who:

- Wear more than one hat – be it consultant, psychologist or psychotherapist – so you should expect it to be a mixture of disciplines.
- Are knowledgeable about how people learn, perform and grow.
- Use that knowledge to help both individuals and groups to develop their personality, aspirations and achievements.
- Think in pragmatic, business terms.

We started this project many years ago when we discovered how much we liked working together and found that we could achieve more when we did. Jackie is a classically trained chartered psychologist and Chris is a blend of psychologist, management consultant and psychotherapist.

In writing this book we are trying to bring useful elements of psychology and psychotherapy to everyday organisational life. This is not an academic piece of work, nor is it a conventional management textbook. Over the years we have read a lot of material and tried out an equally large number of approaches. In this book, we are simply keen to share what we think works.

The Book

This book is divided into information and resources.

- We start off by looking at **personality**.
- The next chapter talks about what happens to personality under **pressure**.
- The third chapter is about **relationships**.
- We then talk about **mood**.
- The fifth chapter is a guide to getting **help** and **support**.

At the end of each chapter, we have included a résumé of top tips, each one supported by additional information in the second part of the book, which is a collection of practical **resources**.

You don't need to read the book in order if you don't want to; you can dip into any chapter as and when appropriate.

And it doesn't stop there. Our *Staying Sane in Business* ambition has been to create something that is informative, thought-provoking and practical, so there's lots more material on our website **www.sane.works** – from questionnaires and reading suggestions to web links and even details of the range of courses and seminars we offer. Just sign up for access to all these additional resources. You can also make your own contribution, as the sane.works project is designed to be a library of everyone's favourite material.

Introducing Martha

This isn't the sort of book that needs lots of case studies because we aren't making claims that need to be backed up with reams of data. What we are trying to do is apply the principles of psychology, therapy and counselling in a workplace context. In order to do this we have created a fictional character, Martha. We hope that she will help to illustrate some of the points we make and that you will enjoy following her story. Here is some background information on her for now.

Dr Martha Stewart is 38. She's a scientist and she works for a pharmaceuticals company in research and development, leading a team of professionals from all over the world whose job it is to guide a candidate drug through the early stages of development and on to clinical trials. It's demanding work by its very nature and made more complex by the fact that much of her team is virtual, spread over several countries and cultures, and it's a team that has a finite life. Once a drug has completed all stages of its development and is in production, the team is disbanded and a new one is formed to shepherd another promising compound from the laboratory to the prescribing physician.

Having risen through the ranks over the last ten years, Martha has entered a leadership development programme, which is aimed at growing board-level talent from within her organisation. Apart from the regular cycle of appraisals and the occasional survey exercise aimed at increasing employee engagement, Martha hasn't had much leadership feedback or development over the years. Her company has provided some excellent training but it's pretty much all been technical in nature.

She's open-minded and happy to join the programme, though a little wary of opening up to other people. Clearly focused on task and process, Martha isn't the sort of person who enjoys a vague brief and she wonders exactly what the programme might be all about. She hopes the investment will pay off and that her time will not be wasted.

'Always be yourself,
express yourself,
have faith in yourself,
do not go out and look for
a successful personality
and duplicate it.'

– Bruce Lee –

Just as you have a personality, you also have a shadow! (Photo by DF)

Who are you?

The foundation stone of staying sane, and therefore a useful place for us to start, is with some exploration of who you are and how you came to be like that.

It's a topic that has been the subject of fierce debate for as long as anyone can remember. There are those at one end of the spectrum who believe that we are pretty much wired up from birth (or even before that) and others who just as firmly hold onto the notion that we are completely a product of our environment. All sorts of things are thrown into the mix along the way: politics, philosophy, ethics – you name it.

As with so many things, the truth probably lies somewhere in the middle: we are a complex and ever-changing blend of genetics and learning. Recent advances in neuroscience have shed a great deal of light on how malleable our brains actually are; experience literally re-wires us. However, it has also demonstrated that we are most sensitive to this re-wiring at the earliest stage of our lives.

Let's suppose, then, that a reasonable definition of who you are is the pattern of thoughts, feelings and behaviours that you usually show in particular circumstances and that have remained reasonably consistent over time. Two interesting questions flow from this:

- What are the patterns that *you* notice in *your* thoughts, feelings and behaviours?
- How helpful are they in dealing with the issues that you face at work?

Staying sane in business – and in life in general – is about either getting out of a stuck place or avoiding going there in the first place. Philippa Perry puts this neatly in her little book *How to Stay Sane* in the excellent School of Life series. Philippa argues that for all the complex systems of classifying human misery, the essential split is twofold. You can either lurch from one crisis to the next, living in chaos, or you can rigidly stick to ways of being that may have worked once but no longer serve you well.

Because you picked up this book and have read this far, we can safely assume that you are interested in your own development. If you want to develop, the more you know about yourself, the better you can be at identifying where you are starting from and the distance you may need to travel. It's our belief that pretty much everything starts with self-knowledge.

Let's not get too hung up about how the measurements are done at this stage but let's just accept that you need some information about your basic personal building blocks: how you tend to solve problems, what may happen to you under stress and pressure, the way in which you grew up and have adapted to the major events in your life, and what meaning you are currently making of your world.

We are putting biology to one side here. That's not to say that it's irrelevant because it's true that genes do play a part in who we are. But, despite the growing field of behavioural genetics, the exact role that heredity plays is not yet fully understood. Sure, there is some solid evidence for genetics making a significant contribution to our personal foundation – raw intelligence, introversion/extroversion and the degree to which we are predisposed to emotional stability, but, at the moment, that's about it.

Think of yourself in descriptive terms. This allows you both to get a fix on who you are and also provides the language for you to make reasonably reliable comparisons with other people, because who you are is relative to everyone else.

Personal Architecture

So, if you want to know more about yourself, where do you start? That's what this chapter is all about. Here are some building blocks:

- **Personal narrative** – Start off by thinking about your personal history, your hopes, dreams and aspirations. Who are you? Where have you come from? Where are you going? Looking back, what was growing up like? What was your experience of education? What major life events have shaped you? What achievements are you most proud of?

- **Consider what you attach meaning to** – What meaning do your current hopes and dreams provide for your life and what are the values that are important to you?
- **Think about your values** – What's really important to you? Hard work that is congruent with your values becomes your passion. Hard work that is at odds with your values is simply a source of stress.
- **Explore what motivates you** – What drives and energises you? How do you like to work and in what role and type of organisation? What excites you and what turns you off? You are a whole person, so what interests you outside of work is just as important.
- **Consider your personality** – Think about what happens to your style and approach under pressure.
- **What skills do you possess?** – Not just technical skills, which are often the subject of certification, but also your whole range of life skills.
- **Think about how you get on with other people** – Particularly in terms of your relationships at work. This might be how you prefer to be involved in things; the extent to which you like to be in control, how you feel about being told what to do and whether you prefer opening up to other people or staying quite private.
- **What about solving problems and learning?** – How do you go about either? Maybe you like to put your nose in a book or perhaps you like to learn by doing. Perhaps you are reflective or maybe you like to move on quickly to the next thing once you have accomplished a goal?
- **Lastly, consider your reputation** – If you weren't in the room, what would other people be saying about you?

Let's look at all of these points in more detail.

Personal Narrative

We all have a story about ourselves. Depending on who we are, we may or may not be so comfortable recounting it! You will come across some people who want to tell you all about themselves – sometimes in a level of detail that you don't actually appreciate. There will be others who are a closed book: private people who change the subject quickly when the spotlight swings round onto them.

Nevertheless, we all have some sense of a personal narrative. One senior leader we worked with would start more or less every public speaking event with a description of the part of society that he came from. It was important to him to let his audience know what his father had once done for a living and that it wasn't a middle-class profession. Whilst it was a badge of honour to him that he had achieved his success in life without a particularly privileged start, in some ways his frequent references to his lowly beginnings also limited his impact. Another CEO once told us that, despite his great success in life, he still clung on to the belief that this was all the more remarkable for someone who came from his geographic part of the UK!

Some schools of psychology go so far as calling this story a life script. If this is true, your script becomes the lens through which you experience your life and the reason why the patterns of your life play out the way that they do. Some scripts are helpful but some are destructive. Scripts sit in the edge of your consciousness, just out of awareness, and like an image out of the corner of your eye, they seem to fade when you look at them directly.

The argument is that scripts were formed early on in your existence and they have a child-like or black-and-white quality about them in their purest form. The way that they play out in your adult self is complex but they do seem to influence the experiences that you seek in life. All scripts can be changed; all narratives can be re-written but first you need to discover what they are.

Here are just four examples of scripts that tend to appear in a workplace context and that could hold you back; of course, there are many more.

- **I always put other people first** – This script is a blocker to you looking after yourself. This could mean not fulfilling your emotional needs, your desire to be recognised, rewarded and promoted, and it might mean not looking after your own health. This script is fuelled by a belief that says, 'Please others and you'll be okay'. This script is slightly more common in women than men, probably as result of upbringing. It's also common in middle managers with large teams of people reporting to them; jobs with a very high set of operational demands. If you have this script, it could be a barrier to coaching and personal development, both of which you might think of as being a bit self-indulgent!

- **I'm never good enough** – This one either exists in its pure form or comes in disguise. The disguised version is more like, 'I'm only as good as my last project or the most recent deal I have closed' or the rather self-limiting statement that 'People like me don't get...'. At its extreme, this makes you strive for more and more to try to counteract the empty feeling within. Sadly, organisations can fuel this belief in the performance management systems they set up. The reward for a stellar year of performance may be a bonus, a pay rise or a promotion but this will nearly always be coupled with even more stretching objectives for the following year. Kept in perspective, this can be no bad thing but if you allow the totality of your identity to be associated with accomplishment, you will never enjoy much mental peace. If you have this script you'll either under-achieve, as you give up before you have started, or you'll anxiously over-achieve and burn yourself out in the process. Either way, you will arrive in coaching or development sessions asking what the process can do to make you more effective and you might not be so keen on stopping and reflecting on the part that you need to play.

- **I always get left out** – An early script about abandonment, in business you could be the person on the edge of social groups, the one who is waiting to be invited rather than the one who does the inviting. If you are in sales, it could be this script that sits behind your fear of initiating new business contacts. This script can drive jealous and possessive behaviour and make you a difficult colleague to work with.

- **Bad things always happen to me** – This one is often about fear of making mistakes. It's sometimes associated with a belief that you must be perfect: a sense that you are only really acceptable if you do not make an error and that any mistake made could well have catastrophic consequences. If you have this script, it's hard for you to try out new things or to simply have a go.

As you can see, these scripts have a grandiose quality about them. Child-like beliefs usually do, and the emphasis here is on child-like not childish. It's easy to spot anything of this nature as the governing thought lacks balance and very often includes words like 'never' and 'always'.

Although we have listed your personal narrative as our first dimension of personal architecture, it's common that a deep understanding of this is arrived at over time. This is a frequent finding in therapy and sometimes in coaching. Clients talk of finding themselves or, even more tellingly, of meeting themselves. Nevertheless, starting the enquiry into who you are at this point makes a lot of sense.

Meaning

Having meaning in our lives is extremely important. In Nazi Germany in the 1940s, it was recognised that the way in which a person framed the experience of being in a concentration camp was a partial determinant of whether or not they survived.

Viktor Frankl's description of this in *Man's Search for Meaning* spawned a whole branch of therapy called Logotherapy, which holds that our primary motivation is to find a meaning in life. Whilst most of us will never have to face anything as harrowing as that which Frankl experienced, the sense we make of our life and what it means is critical to our mental wellbeing.

We need some way of defining ourselves and describing why we are here. We could turn to philosophy or religion, but what interests us is the contribution of psychology.

Most of you will no doubt be familiar with the now-famous Hierarchy of Needs from Abraham Maslow. We also find a similar-looking tool to be useful that comes from the world of neurolinguistic programming, or NLP. It's called Logical Levels and was created by a therapist called Robert Dilts. We use this a lot in coaching to help people who have become stuck with limiting beliefs.

Logical levels – after Robert Dilts

Let's say that you have had enough of your current job and you have a nagging desire to do something else. You decide to use the services of a career coach to explore different options but as you sit down to your very first session you realise with a heavy heart that you have a huge and crippling belief that you just can't change: you have trained too long to do what you are doing; your spouse is very attached to the security that your income brings; much of your identity is wrapped up in your career and the road to re-training looks long and arduous. Change just feels too difficult and you are frustrated and stuck.

Piece by piece, you work with your coach to examine your beliefs. She does this by putting six cards on the floor in front of you, labelled with the six logical levels in the diagram on the previous page. Let's have a go now. Imagine you are doing this exercise. You consider each level in turn. See what conclusions you draw. They can often be very illuminating.

- **Environment: where? when?** – You realise that your decision is partially influenced by timing. Whilst now might not be a perfect time, next year will not be so difficult. One of your children will have left education and your mortgage will be paid off. You have just looked at the layer called Environment in the Logical Levels model.

- **Behaviour: what?** – The job you are doing now isn't that different in some respects from what you want to do. At the level of Behaviour, you won't need to learn many new skills. Some re-training is necessary but you'll be able to take it in your stride.

- **Capabilities: how?** – You also reflect that the core Capabilities of the new role are things that have been mentioned countless times as things that you have the potential to do. It's just that your current job doesn't really call on them.

- **Beliefs and Values: why?** – Going deeper, you acknowledge that you have a strong desire to help people and that this is congruent with your Value that giving something back to society is a very good thing. You weigh this up against the loss of financial security and you realise the potential gain in job satisfaction is greater than the financial loss that you are going to incur. You have a clear rationale for what you are thinking about doing.

- **Identity: who?** – Arriving at the card labelled Identity, you hesitate. You have been working for your current organisation since graduating. It's what you tell people when they first meet you; they recognise your employer as a household name. In your heart though, your desire is to start your own business and for this business to have a pro-social theme to it. Your coach asks you who else you know who has done this and if you identify with them. On reflection, you think of someone in your circle and you conclude that they aren't that different from you and that if they could make a go of it, so could you.

- **Mission: why?** – You'll notice that the levels often become harder to answer the nearer you go to the top. It can feel a bit existential when you start to ask who you are and unnervingly evangelical when you try to describe your life mission. Nevertheless, when we are coaching, we notice that the people who can put a clear label at the very top of their pyramid seem to be the most satisfied and productive individuals that we work with. This can't be an accident!

Later in this book, we talk about resilience and it also seems true to us that a clear mission and sense of purpose in life is one of the critical ingredients in being able to withstand both everyday setbacks and also the bigger disappointments and losses that can happen from time to time.

Values

Then, there's the whole area of values. These days, most organisations have clear sets of values and these are often given a high level of prominence in their promotional literature. Stating what an organisation stands for can be a helpful way of achieving brand differentiation. Knowing what you stand for and how well that matches the values of an organisation can help you decide to join it or stay in it – or not.

They do. Whether you are a business or an individual, values matter. (Photo by CW)

So what about your own values? We don't mean the various ways that authority figures, society, religion or politics tell you how you can live your life in a 'good' or 'bad' way. What 'values' refers to here are those things that you want your life to be about.

It can often be helpful to explore your values by asking yourself what *you* want your life to stand for. If your life could be about something, what would that thing be? Or it could be more than one thing. An enquiry of this nature can be radical and challenging – in fact, it really should be.

Again, remember that you exist in context, in environments and cultures (both in work and, more generally, in society) that reward you for acting and thinking in certain ways. Over time, these patterns of thinking and behaving can become increasingly ingrained, but that doesn't mean that those ways of thinking and behaving reflect your values. In fact, you might feel unhappy, or uncomfortable in some way, in your day-to-day life, as though you aren't living in a way that is consistent with how you really see things and how you want to be.

A social psychologist called Leon Festinger called this 'cognitive dissonance' – the discomfort that arises from knowing that there is inconsistency between your thoughts and behaviour. He suggested that people feel an innate urge to correct such dissonance by altering or dropping one or both of the conflicting ways of thinking and/or behaving. In this way, you 'bend' the evidence to make yourself feel better.

Let's clarify this with a simple example. You buy a sports car that you have been wanting for years. After a few weeks of driving the car, you become aware that it has its good points and its drawbacks. The boot is small, the suspension is rock hard and you don't actually find the driving experience that comfortable. Since it cost you a fortune, you downplay the negative aspects of your chosen vehicle, as you tell your friends in the bar that you own an 'uncompromising marque' and that a few minor disadvantages are a small price to pay for 'engineering excellence'. Your friends stay quiet as they notice you are trying a bit too hard to justify your purchase!

Now try this with your career – an inherently more complex set of decisions and investments than a simple car purchase. You might be competitive, individualistic, freethinking and creative, compassionate, revolutionary or a host of other attributes. Just as it's important to know what you are, it's equally as important to work in an environment and culture in which these aspects of you are welcomed and where you can be the best version of yourself without having to engage in endless compromise.

Once you are clear about your values, it will be easier to identify which patterns of thinking and behaviour are dissonant with them. From there, you can set goals to behave in ways that are consistent with your values.

Assuming there is a dissonance to begin with, this new behaviour is likely to lead to reduced discomfort and unhappiness on a day-to-day basis, and to greater contentment – something that is key to your physical and psychological health.

Motivation

This is a really interesting area as there are many more facets to it than you might at first think. Quite often in business we talk about people being motivated or not, as if it's a simple on/off switch. We seek out motivated people to work for us and we like the thought that other people will see us as switched on and energetic.

But what exactly are you motivated by? There's also the consideration of where and when and, probably, with whom?

Over the years, psychologists have built up a rich picture of human motivation. They like to talk of needs. Lots of needs have been identified but we notice some of them cropping up time and time again. Here are the definitions that we think are most useful:

Human Needs

Need	Characteristics
Achievement	This is all about setting stretching goals for yourself. Sometimes this comes out as competitiveness towards others and sometimes it's all about high personal standards. (Watch out for fear of failure here. We think that's something different.) A strong need for achievement is something we look for as business psychologists when we are assessing people for senior roles. Within reason, it's something that's desirable, if not essential, if you want to reach the top of your profession.
Affiliation	This is the need to belong to a group or something that is bigger than you. It could be a faith, a football team or a project team. Some people are natural 'joiners' whilst some don't feel that comfortable in groups. The need for affiliation is a tough one. In one sense it can make you 'one of the gang' but it's not so useful when you are promoted from within your peer group and you have to make decisions about the people who used to be your friends. All of a sudden, life can feel very lonely.
Power	This is where you experience satisfaction by seeing your environment move in the direction that you want it to. On the one hand this is good, as you will be the captain of your own destiny and the author of your own script. On the other hand, an excessive need for power can be very damaging and corrupting. We have all seen the consequences.
Recognition	We all need to be recognised to one extent or another. Therapists sometimes talk about 'strokes', which are just units of recognition. For some of us, a regular supply of strokes is very significant; for others, less so. If you want a lot of recognition, it's wise to ask yourself how you are getting your needs met. We don't always choose the ways that are best for us.

Need	Characteristics
Security	This is all about feeling safe. It's not necessarily connected with the desire for a quiet life but it is about the absence of threat.
Variety	The spice of life? If so, you have a need for novelty and stimulation. This is the territory of the low boredom threshold and there's some connection here with our propensity to take risks.
Freedom	Experiencing independence and spontaneity is what this one is all about. If you have this need it's likely that you will find rules and procedures to be something of an irritant and you won't always react positively to being told what to do.
Growth	Some of us are only really satisfied if we are learning. Such people love to master a new skill or get their head round a novel concept. There's a lot of evidence that taking the time to learn new things (and it probably doesn't matter what) is an essential component of emotional health, particularly as we age.
Purpose	A little bit like recognition, this one, in that we all need some meaning in our lives. Whilst most of us tire quickly of pointless tasks, for some people this need is much greater as they look for a personal mission and a calling. This is another need that seems to become more prominent as our lives move into middle age and beyond.

Remember, it's very easy for us either to behave as if we are motivated by something because we think that's the right thing to do, or to unwittingly import the motivations of others without realising it. We'd argue that sanity is about living our own dreams and recognising where these differ from the dreams of others.

Before we leave the area of motivation, we'd like to touch on something that therapists often call psychological hungers. The argument goes that just as we get hungry for food and thirsty for water, we also experience the need for nourishment of other kinds. Deprived of these needs, we fail to thrive. So, in addition to the needs above, we also have the hunger for other elements.

- **Contact** – The physical connection you have with other people and the needs that you have to be physically touched have been shown in many experiments to be vitally important.
- **Sex** – It can have an impact on your mental and physical health when you fail to have your needs met in this area.
- **Structure** – This relates to the way in which you carve up your time. There's more about this in Chapter 3, where we look at relationships and how we form attachments to other people.

Personality

Having thought about all these elements, you could then turn your attention to personality.

Curiously, models of personality and their attendant questionnaires seem to attract their own band of loyal followers. In truth, as long as they have been put together with some care, they are all quite similar – it boils down to style as much as anything. Some questionnaires have been designed for the corporate market, some have a developmental twist, some have clinical roots and all of them say as much about their authors as they say about the people responding to them.

One useful way of thinking about personality is to consider the biggest building blocks or main areas to identify. This is where a model called the 'big five' comes in.

The Big Five Personality Model

Personality	Characteristics
Openness to experience	This element covers imagination, aesthetics, openness to feelings, engaging in new activities, exploring new ideas and entertaining the idea that there are lots of different ways to lead your life.
Conscientiousness	This is not just about being ordered, methodical and checking the details but also about self-belief, duty, striving for achievement, exercising self-discipline, and minimisation of risk.
Extraversion	This isn't just about being the life and soul of the party. It's fundamentally about where your level of mental arousal comes from. For extroverts, it's from outside stimulation. For introverts, it's from within and too much external stimulation can be overwhelming.
Agreeableness	Sometimes confused with extraversion, this is actually more about trust, altruism, promoting harmony, showing modesty and experiencing compassion.
Emotional stability	How we deal with the ups and downs of life is considered here, whether or not we experience worry and frustration, the extent to which we often feel down and despondent, how self-conscious we are and how much we can resist our impulses.

There used to be a nice little mnemonic for remembering this: OCEAN. That was when what is now more accurately called Emotional Stability was labelled as Neuroticism.

The advantage of this model is that it has been very well researched over the last thirty years and, as you've probably already worked out, there is a strong connection between personality and success in business. Broadly speaking, for leadership roles it's vital that you are conscientious – in the sense that you are driven to get things done more than to work in a detailed way – and that you are emotionally stable.

It's a bit less important whether you are open to experience, although you'll probably be more amenable to being trained. It also doesn't really matter if you are extraverted or introverted unless your job requires a very large amount of social contact (see *Quiet: The Power of Introverts in a World That Can't Stop Talking* by Susan Cain). You don't even have to be a nice, warm guy or girl, though this can do no harm and would certainly make you more popular!

It's important to remember that personality is not a completely stable concept and it's not 100% predictable. It tends to develop over time, even if some of the components are more resistant to change than others, so the best way to think of it might be as a set of predispositions to behave in certain ways. Personalities bend under pressure and according to our moods, and different environments reward or punish different aspects of them.

Your Skills

At some point in your career, you will need to take stock of what you are really good at. It might be that as you read this book, you are planning a change of direction, or perhaps you are helping someone else make this sort of decision. Start by defining what it is that you are good at or could be good at with more practice. Sometimes, when we are helping clients describe their skills, we encounter some unhelpful modesty! When asked, they either look blank or give such generic answers that their true talents are masked by vanilla corporate language. If you don't know how to define your skills, here are a couple of techniques.

Using Sort Cards to Define Your Skills

One way of stepping back and looking at your skills is to use a set of sort cards. Each card contains a description of a discrete skill. There are plenty of sets on the market that are written in clear and accessible language. All you do is sort the cards into three piles which represent things that you are really good at, things that you do about as well as most other people and things that just aren't you. This little exercise can be really helpful in getting you beyond the constraints of job titles. For example, being an accountant isn't all about numbers, it's as much about processes, logic and social skills. You'll find some recommendations for tools like the sort cards at **www.sane.works**

Using the Johari Window

Another way of understanding what your skills are is to ask other people. But remember, what you ask and how you hear what comes back depends on your frame of reference, how comfortable you are with asking and how much they want to disclose. It also depends on the insight of who is being asked!

There's a useful framework for getting feedback. It's called the Johari Window and it once featured in a complex statement made by then US Secretary of Defense, Donald Rumsfeld, who said in 2002:

> *Reports that say that something hasn't happened are always interesting to me, because as we know, there are known knowns; there are things we know we know. We also know there are known unknowns; that is to say we know there are some things we do not know. But there are also unknown unknowns – the ones we don't know we don't know. And if one looks throughout the history of our country and other free countries, it is the latter category that tend to be the difficult ones.*

Although Rumsfeld was talking about matters of state, the mental model he was using is just as applicable to personal discovery. And what he was describing is much better shown as a diagram:

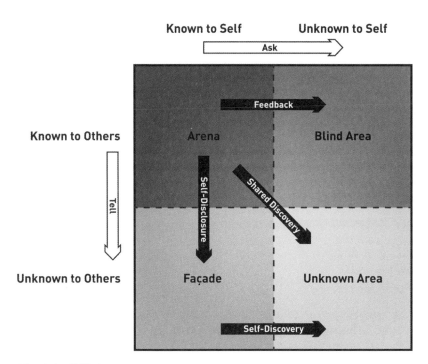

The Johari Window

When we are looking to find out about ourselves, there's:

- Stuff that everyone knows and accepts. This is the open area or **Arena**.

- Things that we know about ourselves but other people don't. A good example is the seemingly cool and calm person who feels really nervous inside but doesn't show it. This is the hidden area or the **Façade**.

- Aspects of who we are that are more apparent to other people than they are to us. Indeed, we might be quite unaware of them. This is our **Blind Area**.

- Stuff that other people don't know about us and nor do we. This is clearly the **Unknown Area**.

To learn more about our skills or, in fact, to learn about pretty much any aspect of ourselves, we can use the Johari Window as follows:

- We could make sure that as much of ourselves as is appropriate goes into the Arena.
- We could shrink or lower the Façade by self-disclosure and where we feel resistant to doing this, we could explore the reasons why.
- We could reduce the Blind Area by asking the right people the right questions and paying careful attention to what we hear. This is feedback.
- We could engage in activities that shed light on aspects of ourselves that other people don't know about and that we keep hidden from ourselves, i.e. the Unknown Area. You could argue that this is very much the territory of deep coaching and psychotherapy.

Relationships

The whole area of relationships gets more attention in Chapter 3. At this point, it might just be useful to think about what your basic attitude is to sharing aspects of yourself with others and how you react when they share aspects of themselves with you; how you seek to control people or experience being controlled by them; and the extent to which you like to be in groups and included or to be left to your own devices.

What's also important is how you form attachments and what being attached to other people feels like. The way in which you formed attachments early on in your childhood tends to repeat throughout your life, and many dysfunctional aspects of adult behaviour can be traced back to a failure to have had relational needs met before we could even speak. More about this later.

Problem Solving

Make the best use of your intellect. (Photo by DF)

Fundamentally, staying sane means making the best use of your intellect and not getting out of your depth. But it's not just about raw horsepower – and let's not get simplistic here either, as psychologists have argued for up to fourteen different types of intelligence, including emotional, creative, musical and intrapersonal (knowing yourself)!

We find the following broad categories helpful.

- **Complexity** – The first is all about you being able to deal with complexity. If you do not have enough raw processing power in this respect, you will either underestimate the size of a problem or you will freeze and fail to take action. It's no better with too much intellect, either. This is where the fine mind is set loose on a problem only to create a solution that is of such Byzantine complexity that it's unworkable.

- **Adaptability** – This is the second way of looking at problem solving and implies choice, your ability to see problems from different angles and the mental agility to do something differently according to the demands of the situation. What sits behind a lot of adaptability is self-confidence.

- **Self-awareness** – The third component of problem solving is all about being in touch at any given moment with what you are thinking, feeling and doing. Knowing what you are doing is fairly straightforward but really understanding what your pattern of beliefs is or being fully in tune with your feelings is less common. Hence, our ability every now and again to catch ourselves out and to say, 'Whatever came over me?'

It's also important to think about problem-solving styles. You might have a distinct preference for logic or intuition. It could be that you only really feel comfortable with the hard facts of what you can see, hear, feel or touch and you like to use a clear process or procedure when you are trying to work something out.

On the other hand, you might be more attracted to using gut instinct or intuition. If this is the case, you'll work better without procedures and processes and you might be particularly pleased about doing something new or untried.

Each approach comes with its strengths, and is more suitable for some tasks than others. It's not uncommon that you will be good at both and there's lots of evidence that they correlate. It's sometimes a matter of choice as much as anything. Chances are though that you will tend to default to one style over the other.

Ask yourself these questions.

- What kinds of problems do you think your dominant or default style would suit, or not suit?
- Think of a current problem at work, or a recent problem you've experienced. Did you neglect either logic or intuition?
- What would it have been like if you had deliberately chosen to adopt the other style to the one you used?
- How can you exercise mindful choice in the future?

Reputation

Organisational life is replete with feedback mechanisms and, with all the 'likes' on Facebook and other social media, you might argue so is your private time!

On the whole, though, anything that sheds some light on the way people see us is a good thing. Getting some reference points regarding how you come across is a great way of taking a reality check, but you do need to remember that the opinions of others are just opinions. How you are perceived tells you as much about the observer as it does about you!

To understand your reputation you could simply ask. You could also gain a structured understanding of how you measure up against criteria that are important in your organisation through 360° feedback.

There's even the idea that you could consider yourself as a brand. Have a think about your favourite brands – whether that's Aldi or Apple, B&Q or BMW, they all mean something to you. They have enduring and consistent characteristics and your connection with them is as much emotional as it is rational. A personal brand that works is a true encapsulation of who you are – not a chimera or false and flimsy façade but something that makes you uniquely memorable for who you truly are. Later, we'll talk about how relationships rely to an extent on consistency and all that you are doing when you pay attention to your own brand is bringing the essence of you to the fore. There's lots of information about personal branding on the web and a good place to start is Jennifer Holloway's book *Personal Branding for Brits* (assuming you are a Brit, of course!).

The Process of Self-Discovery

What we are arguing is that understanding yourself is the first step to ensuring that you stay sane. It's not about attaching a label round your neck – that can be very unhelpful and self-limiting. But a stable sense of who you are is vital for emotional wellbeing and, as we said, it can be the starting point for self-development.

Having talked about some of the dimensions that you could use to explore who you are, how should you actually go about it? One way is to have a developmental assessment session with a business psychologist – someone like one of the authors! There are lots of advantages to this but it's not the only way. Armed with the concepts we have examined in this chapter, you could also simply cultivate the habits of reflective learning and self-observation.

Reflective Learning

Educational theorist David Kolb believed that in order for us to learn information and skills at a deeper level – so that we can flexibly apply those skills to new, challenging situations – we have to engage in a cycle of reflection. This cycle focuses on reflection and learning as cognitive processes; in other words, it describes the things people must do mentally to be able to learn at a deeper level, and apply what they've learnt to new situations and problems. Here's Kolb's model:

Kolb's Cycle of Reflection.

In order to engage in this cycle, you must first have a 'concrete' or real-world experience, either by doing something, listening to someone teach, or by watching someone else do something.

You, the learner, must then reflect on this experience. Ask yourself the following questions next time you have an experience that involves a new skill or concept.

- What skills, behaviour and knowledge did the other person, teacher or I demonstrate? What exactly did they or I do and say? Get the specifics.
- What concepts, theories or practices were called upon? Do I feel I'm aware of those concepts, theories and practices?

- Do any of them not make sense to me? Do I feel that I have an incomplete understanding of what was underpinning what was said or done? Where can I find out more about these?

Following this part of the process, what you then need to do is engage in 'abstract conceptualisation'. This is where you apply those concepts, theories and practices in your mind to your own work. Perhaps picture in your mind's eye what it would look like to apply those to an area of your work by considering these questions in relation to that image.

- What specific concepts or principles that you've learned would you apply?
- What would that look like? What would you be doing? How would you do it?
- How would you know you'd done it right? What would the result be?
- How would you know if you could improve your skills or knowledge? What would indicate that?

The last part involves actually trying out these new concepts and practices in a real-world situation. This is active experimentation. A crucial part is considering the process and results of what you did.

- What did I do? What did I hope that would achieve?
- How did that work out? Did I get the result I had hoped for?
- If I did, was it because I applied the concepts or practices correctly, or for another serendipitous reason? If I did it correctly, how could I apply this effectively again?

You then repeat the cycle, carrying out the steps again to refine your knowledge and skills, using reflection, abstract conceptualisation and real-world experience to increase your performance.

You can enter this cycle at any point, but crucial to the learning process is that you undergo all stages of the cycle in order for deep, meaningful learning to have taken place.

Self-Observation

This is a bit like stepping back and looking at yourself from a distance. We talk about it later when we discuss the importance of recognising and working with mood. A lot of self-observation has its roots in therapy and its current expression in the idea of mindfulness, something we return to later in the book. There are a number of techniques that can help you step out of yourself and take an impartial view of what's happening.

To begin with, you can start building up your skills in self-observation by stopping whatever you are doing and asking yourself the following questions.

- **What specifically am I doing?** – The best way to do this is to describe what someone else would see if they were watching what you are doing.
- **What am I thinking at this point?** – What's my internal narrative saying?
- **What am I feeling?** – It has long been argued that the number of emotions that we can feel is finite. Let's say there are eight and they are: trust, fear, surprise, sadness, disgust, anger, anticipation and joy. Ask yourself, which one am I experiencing? Be true to yourself, some emotions will sit more comfortably with you than others. Since you can only feel through your body, a good tip here is to tune into bodily sensations.
- **How am I breathing?** – The pattern of our breath is a shortcut to our emotional state. (We deal with this in more depth in Chapter 4.)

Having arrived at something of a starting point, where do you go from there? If you can get a fix on the basic building blocks of who you are, you could go on to explore what happens to you under pressure. Your response to challenge can tell you a lot more about how you are constructed and how you got to be you.

Playing to Your Strengths

The idea that you can do anything is misplaced. There are some things that come easier than others and nobody can do everything equally as well.

And what's really helpful is to get a fix on the difference between what you *can do* and you are *cut out to do*.

Let's say you're thinking at this point about everything we have discussed so far and you conclude that you are really good at something. It might be that this is because you always found this skill easy or it might be that you've really had to work at it and that in the beginning you weren't that good. The same applies to something that you are currently finding really hard. Perhaps this isn't your thing or maybe you've had very little chance to practise?

The next section will talk about self-acceptance but overall we think that staying sane is often about knowing the difference between what you *can do* and what you are *cut out to do* and that involves important decisions. So in all the explanation of who you are we invite you to always:

- Identify, work with and play to your natural strengths.
- Explore and nurture your potential.
- Accept where you have developed coping strategies for things that you are weak at.
- Seriously consider getting other people to do the things that you are not good at and – no matter how hard you try – you don't seem to improve.

Of course, if you turn this on its head you end up with a situation that feels a lot less sane! Imagine not getting the opportunity to play to your strengths or develop your potential. Worse still, imagine putting all of your effort into trying to get better at something you can only just get by in or that you are simply not cut out to do. If one of the authors of this book had been judged by his abilities in football and woodwork and if he had attached much importance to either, his experience of education would have been very different!

The Power of Self-Acceptance

Whatever you conclude as you think about who you are, be flexible in your response to it and bear in mind that all change involves effort and that circumstances dictate desired directions. Try and create a plan for your personal development that doesn't read like a charge sheet that contains everything you are poor at. Work with the resources and time that you have available, with the grain of your personality and abilities and consider where you will extract the maximum return on your investments.

Martha's Starting Point

Martha's leadership programme started with self-knowledge, and the first step was a full assessment with a business psychologist who was also to be her coach for the next six months.

Martha approached her assessment with some scepticism. She'd never filled in psychometric questionnaires before and she was curious what they would tell her that she didn't already know. She also wondered quite what she'd be talking about for three hours to a relative stranger! In the event, the questionnaires weren't difficult to complete but it was the assessment meeting that really surprised her – in a good way. Expecting to be required to 'jump through hoops', what Martha actually experienced was a warm, supportive and intriguing conversation and one that really made her stop and think.

A week after her meeting with the psychologist, Martha received her report and the recommendations for tailoring the leadership programme to her needs. What she discovered was that she was not only rather a driven person but also that under pressure she had a tendency to become brittle and difficult to please and would often retreat into a private world in which she ruminated on her mistakes. Well respected as she was, she recalled feedback on more than one occasion from various well-meaning colleagues, who had said that she was a harsh self-critic and that this seemed to make her tense, demanding and a challenge to get on with.

Martha also recognised that she was often better at the start of a project than in the later stages and that she didn't deal with conflict very well. Given that she had no direct line control over the teams she led, influencing people indirectly always felt a struggle. Whilst she was warm and affable enough, she accepted that being a figurehead took its toll and made her relish time on her own, time that she seldom got.

Martha felt ambitious but it was clear that she also felt confused. Her job didn't require as much technical input as it once had and she was finding it hard to let go of that aspect. She couldn't quite decide whether she was a manager or a scientist, and with a wry smile she recalled the time when she used to question what the purpose of leadership was. Blushing slightly during the assessment session, she confessed to her coach that she had once said to a friend that management was nothing more than telling people what to do! Another slightly painful admission for Martha was that she has made a few political missteps over the past couple of years and that she had off-sided some important stakeholders.

It was also clear that Martha wasn't brilliant at slowing down and, if anything, expected everyone else to keep up with her frenetic pace. The feedback from other people, which formed part of the assessment, was quite telling. Martha's self-image was of being a clear, crisp and timely communicator. Her virtual team was less convinced. Some of them were on her wavelength but others found her vague and confusing. Overall, she seemed better on transmit than receive, and it made her stop and think when she realised that several of the people she was regularly in contact with wanted her to pay more attention to what they were saying.

Martha was invited to sit with her report and the psychometrics for a week and then meet her coach for a second time to pull together a contract for her development. Martha's contract had three broad aims:

- To improve her communication skills.
- To help her deal more effectively with conflict.
- To enhance her political awareness and ability to influence people indirectly.

Together, Martha and her coach talked about what needed to be done and how they were going to make progress. The decision was made to meet at monthly intervals for two hours, off-site, and for email and phone contact in between.

Top Tips for Getting to Know Yourself Better

- Take some time to write down your personal narrative.
- Reflect on what you feel to be your purpose in life.
- Do a personal stock-take of all the skills and experience that you have.
- Reflect on your motivations.
- Learn more about your personality.
- Think about how you tend to relate to others and how you form relationships.
- Watch yourself solve a workplace problem and think about your preferred style.
- Get some feedback.
- Cultivate the skill of self-observation.
- Ask for development assessment if your organisation offers this.

Don't forget – there's more information for each tip in **Part 2** (see pages 191–215) of this book and online at **www.sane.works**

'Many of us feel stress
and get overwhelmed
not because we're taking on
too much, but because we're
taking on too little of what
really strengthens us.'

– Marcus Buckingham –

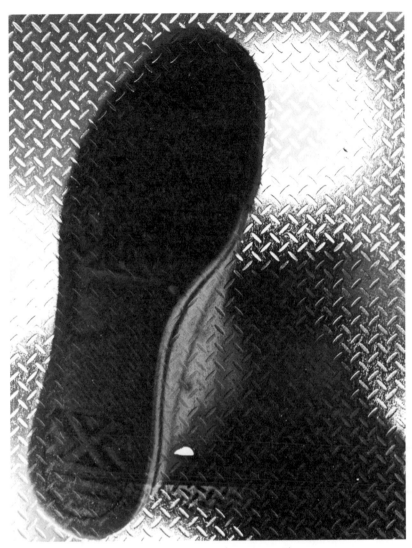

Under pressure our personalities change. (Photo by DF)

Avoiding Autopilot

This is not a book about stress management. For one thing, we think the media focus on 'stress' is misguided and misleading. The dictionary definition of stress is 'mental, emotional or physical strain or tension'. But it is not the tension that is the important element in a work context. It's an abstraction that isn't helpful. What is important is the unique way each of us reacts and adapts to pressure and the consequences that flow from this.

So, what happens when the demands of a situation exceed your ability to cope? What do you think? How do you feel? What do you do?

The last chapter was drawn a great deal from the world of business psychology. The ones that follow are more closely connected with psychotherapy. If Chapter 1 was about knowing yourself and understanding your starting point, the remainder of the book is about helping you to take control, to make positive choices and avoid a life lived on mental autopilot.

The problem is that we all have a tendency to resort to familiar ways of coping, and this is emphasised when we are under pressure because that makes us feel as though there is less scope for acting differently.

This chapter looks at personality under pressure. We talk about the primary ways in which you deal with pressure, your psychological drivers, some of the rules for living that you learned when you were growing up, and a number of ways in which you can counteract this early programming if it's not helping you anymore.

Instinctive Safety Strategies

Under pressure, we act to stay safe. That's because the mind's 'threat system' kicks in; your brain senses that you may be in trouble and in response it uses a system that human beings have developed through many thousands of years of evolution. We will look at this in more detail when we go on to consider relationships.

This response system is designed to keep you from danger by helping you to fight off, run away from (flight), or freeze in the presence of whatever it is that is threatening you. In prehistoric times, this may actually have been a predator or a truly life-threatening situation. However, in the modern day we still carry around this system relatively unchanged. So when you encounter a challenging, high-pressure situation – for example, a deadline that needs to be met, or a confrontation with a colleague – this same system instinctively kicks in. The system attempts to prepare you for the threat in one of three different ways – fight, flight or freeze – influencing the way you think, feel and behave.

- **Fight** – Under significant pressure to meet an unrealistic deadline, you may jump into fight mode. You may think you are being treated unfairly; you may feel angry and upset; perhaps you raise your voice and make demands for the deadline to be extended. This may be all very well in evolutionary terms but in the context of a modern business … possibly career-limiting!

- **Flight** – What if you enter into coaching, knowing that you have some skeletons in the cupboard: things that you know you really should face up to but you find it hard to do so? What if your coach helps you explore these but, faced with tackling them, you psychologically run away and cancel all the rest of your sessions?

- **Freeze** – Say you grew up in a family environment where you had to keep quiet in order to stay out of trouble. In high-pressure situations, you are likely to use the same tactic and keep your opinions and needs to yourself. You might think, 'If I give my opinion, people might get angry or ridicule me'. Afterwards you feel upset, and reflect that you didn't stand up for yourself. Maybe later you develop low self-esteem. This could be equally career-limiting.

What is important here is that, under the influence of this system, we all develop particular safety strategies which are crafted by our earlier experiences and previous learning. Sometimes these are adaptive and helpful for the task at hand; they help us keep quiet when we should, fight our corner when we need to, or escape a situation that just doesn't feel right. But sometimes, the safety strategy isn't helpful. Sometimes it is past its sell-by date, and was only fit for an environment that no longer exists.

In identifying your own safety strategies when you are under pressure, it can be useful to use the mindfulness techniques we discuss later in this book, to become more psychologically aware of your thoughts, memories, emotions, physical changes and behaviour, and to notice particular patterns. You can then reflect on how these patterns of thinking, feeling and behaving impact on your work and performance.

Your Life Position

You might have heard the phrase 'I'm OK, you're OK'. The book by Thomas Harris has been a best-seller since the late 1960s and has provided over 15 million people with a practical introduction to a branch of psychotherapy founded by Eric Berne, called Transactional Analysis or TA.

Of central importance in TA, and sometimes represented as a simple grid, is the idea of life positions. Berne argued that as we grow up, we start to form convictions about the world we live in and at their simplest these are:

- I'm OK, or
- I'm not OK
- You're OK, or
- You're not OK

Putting these together into their possible combinations we arrive at four, basic positions.

- I'm OK, you're OK.
- I'm not OK, you're OK.
- I'm OK, you're not OK.
- I'm not OK, you're not OK.

The first position (I'm OK, you're OK) is the most desirable, the healthiest and the most productive way to live in the world. We argue that this is the sanest position of all! Therapists would say that this is really what their work is aimed at achieving.

The third position is one-up over everyone else, or at least most people. We look at this later when we discuss difficult personalities. The fourth position is one where everything seems hopeless.

It's the second position (I'm not OK, you're OK) that we really want to explore in this chapter. We all experience the feeling that we aren't OK at some time in our lives, and any situation in which we feel we are being judged – from exams to appraisals – can activate it. Experienced occasionally and in response to specific circumstances, it's pretty normal. The problem happens when we are stuck in this position, where it dominates our way of being and where what we do as a consequence hurts us rather than makes things better.

You first experienced the I'm not OK, you're OK feeling to some extent when you were growing up. After all, as a child, you were in the company of people who were bigger, stronger and hopefully wiser than you. It's at this point, particularly if your upbringing wasn't very supportive or nurturing, that you may have hit upon the idea that you might not be *unconditionally* OK but that you could be so much better in the eyes of others if you were to consistently behave in certain ways.

The difficulty is that what worked for you as a child, is not necessarily an adaptive and helpful thing to do as an adult.

Primary Orientation to Pressure

To explore this a bit more, think about a major challenge that you recently faced at work and how you reacted to it.

- Did you become active or passive?
- Did you involve others or withdraw from them?

Being active means that you took the initiative and tried to solve the problem; that you were constructive, rational and solution-focused. Being passive is a bit more complex. It's not just about doing nothing. True, it might mean that you did nothing or waited to be asked, but it also covers any behaviour that didn't actually solve the problem; so it could have been that you over-adapted to someone else's unreasonable demands, you went off sick, you retired to the pub or, worse still, that you picked a fight with someone. Passivity is non-problem-solving behaviour in our view.

Involving others or withdrawing is more straightforward; it's all about whether you asked for help or support, found solace in a group or you went it alone.

So, what did you do and is this what you do most of the time?

- **Actively involved** – Gathering other people around you, maybe taking a lead and encouraging others to talk about what needed to be done.
- **Actively withdrawn** – Deciding that if you wanted the job doing properly you were best doing it yourself as other people didn't have the skills or couldn't be relied upon.
- **Passively involved** – Feeling a bit withdrawn and probably quite rebellious and possibly putting a spanner in the works or at least not being very supportive of others but secretly hoping you would be pulled into group activities.
- **Passively withdrawn** – Where you retreated into the security of your own world and didn't join in with other people or try to solve the problem.

Who's Driving?

Sitting behind the tendencies to act in these broad ways are what we call drivers. Drivers are the direct responses that you settled on early in childhood when you experienced the I'm not OK feeling in relation to adults making you feel vulnerable. These are the OK-if statements. There are five of them.

- **Be perfect** – I'm OK if I don't make mistakes.
- **Be strong** – I'm OK if I don't have any feelings or wants.
- **Try hard** – I'm OK if I try hard (but don't actually do it, because if I did it, I wouldn't be trying hard).
- **Please others** – I'm OK if people are happy with me and like me.
- **Hurry up** – I'm OK if I'm rushing around and operating at pace.

The more love, nurture and acceptance you had as a child, the less these drivers tend to play out. The problem is – in words less graphic than Larkin's 'This Be The Verse' – that parents are never perfect! Somewhere along the line you will have received a number of messages about how you should be and you adapted accordingly. Not all of these messages were supportive and unconditionally accepting of you as a unique individual.

Driver Identification

It's quite easy to spot your drivers. The objective here is not to force yourself to change but rather to become aware of how you are under pressure and to consider if this is how you wish to be.

It's our belief that the way you deal with pressure at work at the moment makes sense to you, has its roots in something that was once adaptive and helpful but that it might not be serving you so well any more. Sanity is not about feeling bad and trying to rush change; it's about self-acceptance and entertaining different possibilities and choices.

Drivers and Associated Behaviours

Driver	Behaviours under pressure	Where it helps	Where it doesn't
Be perfect	Deliberate speech Aloof, stiff body language Compulsive neatness Going into a lot of detail Finger steepling Chin stoking Upright body Eyes up or to the side, not down Tight lipped Talking in parentheses	Organisational skills Plans ahead Prepares thoroughly Accurate Careful with risk Logical	Misses deadlines Overly critical Can't delegate easily Too much detail/ jargon Complex solutions

Be strong	Flat tone	Cool head in a crisis	Delegation is a weakness
	Monotonous	Firm, stands ground	Tendency to over-work
	Few gestures	Sense of duty	Lacks empathy
	Closed body language	Sticks with un-pleasant tasks	Unemotional
	Immobile	Can work well alone	Excessive task focus
	Talks in a way that is cut off from own feelings – externalises things		
Try hard	Tense tone, often muffled	Sticks with hard jobs	Not getting things done
	Many questions	Can be very enthusiastic	Abdicates not delegates
	Hesitant	Innovative	Gets bored easily
	Goes off at tangents	Creative	Pursues own agenda
	Clenched fists	Hard worker	
	Hand by side of head	High performance standards	
	Hunched up, strained		
	Wrinkled brow		
	Talks about 'trying to ...'		
Please others	Smiling, head nodding	Flexible	Conflict averse
	Shows anxiety easily	Adaptable	Sensitive to criticism
	Rising inflection	Sensitive to feelings	Can't say no
	High, squeaky tone	Listens	Not assertive
	Reaches out, palms up	Looks like they care	Rescues others
	Shoulders hunched		
	Leans forward		
	Looks upwards under raised eyebrows		
	Exaggerated smile with bared teeth		

Driver	Behaviours under pressure	Where it helps	Where it doesn't
Hurry up	Staccato speech Fidgets Runs words to-gether Taps fingers Waggles feet Agitated body posture Shifts gaze a lot	Multi-tasks Gets a lot done Agile, thinks quickly Good with deadlines	Makes mistakes Cuts corners Interrupts Doesn't brief clearly

Table adapted from Joines & Stewart, Personality Adaptations, Lifespace, 2008

Adapted Personalities

Personalities change under pressure and the way that you typically adapt has its origins early on in your life. You will probably have a preferred style and the following table illustrates one way of looking at it.

Characteristics of Adapted Personalities

Type	Characteristics	Primary Orientation	Primary drivers
Enthusiastic over-reactor	Excitable Emotionally volatile Over-reacts Dramatic Attention-seeking Seductive	Active – Involving	Please others
Responsible workaholic	Conforming Conscientious	Active – Withdrawing	Be perfect
Brilliant sceptic	Shrewd Rigidity of thought Suspicious Alert for signs of unfairness Prone to retaliation	Between Passive and Active – Withdrawing	Be perfect Be strong

Dreamer	Withdrawn Detached Daydreaming Imaginative	Passive – Withdrawing	Be strong
Charming manipulator	In conflict with society Low tolerance of frustration Need for excitement and risk Relaxed moral code Charming Manipulative Self-serving	Between Active –Involving and Passive – Withdrawing	Please others Be strong
Playful resistor	Focused and outwardly compliant but inwardly non-compliant Procrastination Stubborn Reluctant to work as a team member	Passive – Involving	Try hard

Table adapted from Ware, Personality Adaptations (Doors to Therapy), TAJ 1983 and Vann Joines, Using Redecision Therapy with Different Personality Adaptations, TAJ 1986

You in the Workplace

The idea of the adapted personality has long since transferred from therapy into organisational life. After all, in the table above you can see some distinctly clinical-looking labels! As business psychologists, we are routinely asked about the risk of executive derailment. We are interested in the risk that lies in the overdone strength: the enthusiastic, 'life and soul of the party' who becomes volatile, moody and difficult to please under pressure; the diligent, detailed professional who becomes paralysed by perfectionism, and so on.

The table previously does not include some of the extremes of personality that show up at work. These are really personality disorders and include extreme anti-socials, narcissists, Machiavells, and those with what is now called Hubris Syndrome. There is more on these extremes on pages 107–114.

Staying Sane Under Pressure

Knowing your habitual pattern of response when challenged, pressured or even threatened is as useful as knowing about the basic building blocks of your personality. If you don't want to live on autopilot or to become the victim of your own destructive drivers, this area of self-knowledge is essential. Even better if you can collect some data from what other people say they see you doing when you are really up against it! The more you know about what you actually do as opposed to what you would like to think you do, the better.

But if you are going to stay really sane at work, you need to go one step beyond self-awareness. You need to understand where the more dysfunctional elements of your personality under pressure come from.

The reason why therapists and psychologists are so interested in your formative years is because of the profound impact that they have. The life scripts that are formed early on run the risk of being repeated forever. And not all of these scripts are positive and empowering.

When you were growing up, you received a number of 'parental' messages about how you should be and you incorporated these into your own mind without questioning them. Some of this programming was complete before you could even speak; some came later. If you weren't brought up by your biological parents, then the messages would have come from your primary carers or other important attachment figures. During your teenage years, you inevitably rejected some of this material as you formed your own identity but you kept a surprising amount in your mental attic and what you kept has helped shape who you are.

More than at any other time, this programming plays out when you are under pressure. Before you feel like blaming your parents or caregivers, by the way, it's best to realise that a lot of what was passed on to you was done unintentionally or even unconsciously.

So what exactly were you exposed to?

Back in the 1960s, two therapists called Bob and Mary Goulding described twelve themes that occurred time and time again as the basis for early negative decisions that people made about their lives. For each 'Don't' statement, they asserted that a child would create an OK-if response.

It is these responses that we see being played out time and time again at work and which are brought into sharpest focus when you are under pressure or out of sorts.

- **Don't exist** – Not all of us were born into families where our place was secure, where we were welcomed, nurtured and nourished. A surprisingly large number of very successful people we meet had quite a rough start to their lives, and while many cope very well, for some there remain significant scars. Staying sane seems to us to be very much about accepting your fundamental right to exist and not to have to justify this existence.

- **Don't be you** – This could have been the result of your parents wanting you to be a different gender or personality; sometimes it's about comparison with a sibling or another person. Either way, you grow up with the idea that it is better to be like someone else than to be you.

- **Don't be a child** – This parental message could have been given to you by adults who are not comfortable with small children or who were never properly allowed to be children themselves. You could also consider this message as 'Don't have fun' or 'Don't enjoy yourself'. In some families, fun is not rewarded but is confused with sin or laziness. Being a child, as opposed to being childish, is incredibly important at times. Without permission to be a child, it is very hard to be creative.

- **Don't grow up** – It is often the youngest child who gets this message. Maybe one or both your parents placed great emphasis on being a good mother or good father. Sometimes caregivers who are afraid of being left give this message. Perhaps one of your parents found your growing sexuality as an adolescent disturbing and became distant. You could have interpreted this as it not being OK to be an adult.

- **Don't make it** – Some parents seem to live their lives vicariously, celebrating every success of their children as if it were their own; however, some become jealous. All parents have a child locked inside them, just as you do. That child is capable of feeling jealous even as the adult part of the parent celebrates his or her offspring's success. This confusing message from a parent might make you subconsciously sabotage your own success later in life.

- **Don't (do anything)** – This is all about fear. It's the message that says keep your head down, stay safe and make sure you always have a grown-up looking over you. As a result, you might be waiting for someone to give you permission at work when, in fact, you should be taking action.

- **Don't be important** – If you received this message, you might find it tough when you are called upon to be a leader, when you are promoted and when people start to defer to you. Your response might be to do yourself down, to use a lot of self-deprecating humour or to even make a mess of more senior jobs so you can return to the safety of relative anonymity.

- **Don't belong** – Perhaps you grew up feeling different from the children around you and your parents reinforced this. Perhaps this was connected with race, religion or assumed social status. As a result, you might now find being in certain groups a challenge.

- **Don't be close** – This could have been modelled to you by parents who rarely touched each other or who didn't display physically affectionate behaviour to you. Or perhaps you come from a family where feelings are not spoken about. If this was the case, maybe you now feel suspicious of the motives of others or you feel inclined to destruction-test your relationships to make sure the bonds are real.

- **Don't be well** – There's a secondary benefit with illness: it gets you attention. Maybe you were starved of real love or at least your parents were distracted and unavailable. If you noticed that being unwell got you the much-needed affection that you were craving, maybe you settled on this as a lifelong tactic?

- **Don't think** – If one or more or your parents consistently belittled your thinking, this is the message that you might have received. Your adult response to a pressurised situation that you need to figure your way out of might be to become confused or to substitute feeling for thinking.

- **Don't feel** – If your parents bottled up their feelings, this might be the message that you took on board. Sadly this one particularly applies to males – 'big boys don't cry' is still commonly heard!

These statements can look a bit stark when viewed in isolation, so it's best to remember they are based on the primitive thinking patterns of very small children. For the most part, you will have inferred them, and very few will have actually been articulated.

The problem is that, at some level, you do remember them and they come into play without you really being aware of the impact they have. The more aware you are of what is secretly driving at least some of your behaviour at work, the more resilient you become.

So, in the continued spirit of looking after your sanity, we now turn to what you can do.

Taming the Demons

There are a number of ways you can avoid living on autopilot. They all rest on the idea that you can develop awareness, that you have the power to change and that change can be for your good.

Let's start with your drivers. Once you have become aware of these drivers kicking in, you could hold in mind a disputing statement.

There's a good technique derived from cognitive behavioural therapy that you can use here. It's called the ABCD method.

- **A for activation and awareness** – What's the event that has lead to you thinking or feeling in a specific way and what are you aware of thinking or feeling? What's the narrative that is running through your head and where in your body can you locate the feeling?

- **B for belief and behaviour** – What is it that you believe to be true in this situation? Take 'big boys don't cry', for example. Is this what you really believe to be true? Is this belief limiting you in any way or does it empower you? Then consider what it is that you are actually doing. If you were to step outside of your body and observe your behaviour, what would you see?

- **C for consequences** – When you experience yourself doing what you generally do under pressure, what usually happens? If you keep getting the same results and these results are not what you want, something needs to change.

- **D for dispute** – If you were to hold a different belief, what might the effect be? This is sometimes called reframing. Let's start by looking at how this works in terms of your drivers. Let's say, for example, you are aware that under pressure you tend to run around, frantically trying to please others. What if you slowed your pace slightly and at least brought your own satisfaction into the equation?

At the highest level, you could practise with an antidote.

Antidotes to Unhelpful Drivers

Driver	Antidote statement
Be perfect	You are good enough as you are
Please others	Please yourself
Be strong	Be open and express your wants
Try hard	Do it!
Hurry up	Take your time

Without wishing to be too cheesy, wouldn't it be helpful if you at least wrote these antidote statements down somewhere, so they are handy when you need them? We favour a bit of discretion here as the time may now have passed when putting them on the office wall is seen as a mark of great emotional intelligence. The choice is yours, of course.

You can go beyond developing awareness of your primary orientation to pressure and your drivers, together with their potential antidote statements, and repeat this exercise at the level of your chosen personality adaptation. Here are some suggestions. You might notice that the 'Hurry up' driver is generally one that acts in conjunction with the drivers stated here. So, the compulsion might be to hurry up and please others, hurry up and be perfect etc. Working with antidotes will not only be about acting on the primary driver but also about deliberately slowing down.

Antidotes to Unhelpful Behaviour

Personality adaptation	Antidote practices
Enthusiastic over-reactor Primary driver: Please others	Notice your feelings. Really explore them with someone you are comfortable talking things over with. This isn't somebody who wants to comment on your behaviour. After all, in your mind you are already doing everything you can to keep people happy. If you are angry, explore this feeling more and see if it's sitting behind anxiety. No matter how strong your feelings are, recognise them as just feelings and don't immediately act on them. Explore your thoughts. Try to cultivate a habit of mindfulness and self-acceptance. Engage in thinking as much as feeling and try the ABCD approach. It may have been that your parental messaging was don't think, don't grow up, don't be important or don't be you. These are worth exploring.

Personality adaptation	Antidote practices
Responsible workaholic **Primary driver: Be perfect**	Notice your thoughts. Really explore them with someone you are comfortable talking things over with. This isn't somebody who wants to comment on your behaviour. After all, in your mind you are already doing everything you can to avoid making mistakes. Cultivate loosening up, playing and making the occasional mistake. It's OK to be you. You are already good enough and your best is quite adequate. You don't have to be perfect. There's nothing to be gained by working yourself to death. How does it feel as you explore this? If other people are making you angry through their unreasonable demands, explore this feeling, too; it may be a feeling that you are using to mask something else – maybe anxiety, guilt or depression. It's common that we cover up one feeling with another and feeling cross is often a great deal more palatable than feeling vulnerable. It may have been that your parental messaging was don't be a child, don't be close, don't be important and don't feel. These are worth exploring.
Brilliant sceptic **Primary drivers: Be perfect, Be strong**	Notice your thoughts. Really explore them with someone you have a trusting relationship with and who you feel safe talking things over with. This isn't somebody who wants to comment on your behaviour. After all, in your mind you too are already doing everything you can to avoid making mistakes and you don't like feeling vulnerable either.

(Continued ...) Brilliant sceptic Primary drivers: Be perfect, Be strong	Try and get a reality check on your thoughts. Maybe get some feedback. Are things really as you perceive them to be? Is there another position that you could take or a different frame that you can put on what's happening?
	Take your time. There's no rush and there's no need to be hard on yourself. Be mindful when the 'shoulds', 'oughts' and 'musts' appear in your language. How are you feeling as you say these things?
	It may have been that your parental messaging was don't be a child, don't be close and don't feel. These are worth exploring.
Dreamer Primary driver: Be strong	Notice your behaviours. When do you retreat into your private world? Where do you go and what occupies your thoughts? When are you being passive? Remember passivity is not just doing nothing; it's any non-problem-solving behaviour. Work with a coach or mentor who brings you out of yourself and helps you express your thoughts. Try to avoid working with someone who keeps asking you how you feel!
	Own your feelings and explore asking for what you want and need, rather than running away. If you find yourself saying 'it' rather than 'I', that could be a clue...
	Your needs are as important as those of anyone else. Don't dismiss the possibility of having them met.
	It may have been that your parental messaging was don't think, don't be important, don't feel (especially strong emotions), don't belong, don't grow up and don't be well. These are worth exploring.

Personality adaptation	Antidote practices
Charming manipulator Primary drivers: **Please others, Be strong**	Notice your behaviours. Do you recognise when you are manipulating people to your own ends? Is there a better, more fulfilling way to relate to people? What would you risk if you really trusted someone and let them appreciate you for all that you are? How would you feel if you experienced this? It may have been that your parental messaging was don't think, don't be important, don't be close, don't make it, don't feel (particularly negative emotions) and don't think. These are worth exploring.
Playful resistor Primary driver: **Try hard**	Notice your behaviours. Do you experience being stuck, with different parts of you wanting different things? Or do you find yourself engaged in battles that, if you step back, are actually pointless? How do you relate to authority figures? Try working with a coach who accepts you the way you are and who gives you the space to explore what holds you back, without necessarily insisting that you have clear goals to work on. Choose someone that you can have a bit of fun with. Experiment with stating your needs more. Be direct and ask for what you want and be prepared to say no to what you don't want. Work on your fear of expressing your feelings directly. It may have been that your parental messaging was don't grow up, don't feel, don't enjoy and don't be close. These are worth exploring.

Taking Control of Your Rules for Living

This chapter has been all about how you might think, feel and act under pressure. The way you have adapted to the world is unique to you and always began as a way of being that was designed to protect you. None of us knowingly does anything to damage ourselves and even though some of the tactics you now employ may not be working, it doesn't mean that the initial choice was wrong. Becoming aware of how you react to pressure is the first step to avoid the autopilot effect. It's at this point you can then re-decide.

Remember that we all develop rules for living. These are thoughts that we might not be aware of day to day, but that nonetheless have a big impact on how we choose to behave. They can be considered like unwritten statements about how we should live our lives. We don't agree that it's pressure that makes you 'revert to type' or that stress causes the 'true you' to emerge. What we do think is that pressure causes you to fall back, often unthinkingly, on your own compendium of life rules.

So, if your number one rule for living is 'If I complete all my work to the highest standard, then I am worthwhile as a professional/person' you might want to ask what happens if you make a mistake or what you should do when detailed perfectionism isn't what's needed and a quick and simple solution would suffice.

Some of your rules for living will be perfectly adaptive and helpful; for example, 'If I get most of my work done on time, then I will be appreciated by my manager and colleagues'. See the difference with the perfectionist example? One is flexible, supportive and helpful but still urges you on to better things whilst the other is rigid, punitive and potentially destructive.

If you really want to stay sane in business, be prepared to do some work on yourself. Be curious about how your formative experiences have shaped you and work with a coach or therapist to disentangle the past from the present, the influences that have caused you to be you and, in particular, what you usually do when you get knocked off your even keel.

Psychotherapists, psychologists and many coaches believe that our earliest relationships and experiences are often the most crucial in crafting our ability to know ourselves – our thoughts, emotions, behaviour – and being able to manage our own stress and upset effectively. Our earliest relationships are also often heavily involved in shaping how we relate to others, how we think about the world around us and how we think about our future. (We will explore relationships more in the next chapter.) The difficulty is that a lot of these key events and relationships occurred and formed in early life, so they can also be the most difficult to recall!

However, in reflecting on your own thoughts and memories, you may find that certain ways of thinking seem to link quite logically with repeated memories of early relationships. It may be that those relationships led you to expect certain responses from people, or in some cases to not expect certain responses from people (for example, 'People will be loving towards me' or 'People are unpredictable and hurtful towards me'). They may have logically led you to think about yourself, the world or other people in particular ways as a result.

Often, these beliefs about relationships and the world around us are learned. Ways of thinking about relationships and other people, and the behaviours shaped by these ways of thinking, may have been rewarded by helping you to stay close to others, obtain praise, or avoid punishment (remember that punishment may be getting something negative, but it can also be the withholding of something positive, such as attention and affection as a child).

These beliefs can often give rise to the rules for living we considered above. For example, if I think people are punishing me because as a child I was punished a lot for not doing well in school, I may develop the rule for living that 'if I excel at everything, I am a good person' to try to avoid punishment. The reason this happens is because the rules for living buffer us against the consequences of these beliefs; in the example above, this consequence might be that I will be punished and feel worthless.

What this chapter has been about is the difficultly that comes when these rules are inflexible and demand standards that are impossible to maintain over the longer term. It's like having a highly critical parent lodged inside your head, reminding you that you are never good enough.

The risk is that you will eventually 'burn out' – you may one day be physically and/or emotionally overwhelmed and find it impossible to reach your goals. As a result of your rigid rules being broken, your self-esteem plummets and, to use a word that medics sometimes employ, you become 'acopic', your adaptive energy spent and your enjoyment of life massively diminished. Taken to extremes – and sadly these extremes happen – some people begin to wonder whether it's worth living at all.

Martha's Coaching

Having decided on three focus areas for coaching around communication, conflict and influence, Martha was surprised that her coaching wasn't simply concerned with thinking about better ways of reaching her goals. In truth, she was expecting to learn a set of tools and techniques, and being invited to explore her feelings took her aback. Although she brought some current problems to her session in the hope that she could use the reflective space to puzzle out better solutions and extend her repertoire of skills, she was caught off guard when her coach gently enquired into the way that she coped when the heat was on.

She recalled that as a child her father had been a remote character, often away on business and, even when home, emotionally cool and difficult to reach. Martha's mother had been warmer and more responsive to the immediate needs of her children but her problems with depression also meant that she wasn't always around when needed. Martha and her sister had grown up needing to be strong and self-reliant, and when praise did feature in their lives, it was generally in response to academic attainment. Sport was considered a waste of time, and duty and order reigned supreme in the Stewart household.

Thinking about the way she now behaved at work, Martha concluded that there were clear echoes of the past. No matter how much pressure she was put under, she was reluctant to ask for help. She acknowledged that she was spending most of her time living in her head and that the emotional problems that staff brought to her from time to time caused her to inwardly sigh. Sometimes Martha found that if she wanted something doing it was so much easier to do it herself than involve others.

Towards the end of the coaching session, her coach enquired into Martha's life outside work and tearfully Martha confessed that there was little to tell. The sheer number of hours she worked left little time for anything else and often all that she could do at the end of the working day was flop in front of the TV with a glass of wine. Her social circle had dwindled since her friends had started families and it was over two years since Martha had been in a serious relationship. She loved her job but she wanted more out of life. What seemed to be holding her back was an endless game of 'until' and 'when' that she was playing. She'd just keep this workload up until the current project was over; she'd know that she was doing a good job when she got the promotion that meant so much to her; she'd relax and re-kindle her social life when there was time. As they were finishing off and planning for the next session, Martha's coach asked her to reflect on something. How would Martha know when she was successful? With a slightly dismissive air, Martha exhaled, grabbed her iPhone and carried on her day. This was a question she'd address later ...

Top Tips for Understanding Yourself Under Pressure

- Notice your pattern of response to pressure.
- Consider your derailers – those things that knock you off course.
- Notice your OK-if thoughts or feelings.
- Get a handle on your drivers.
- Reflect on what growing up was like for you.
- Try the ABCD and antidote statement method of taming your drivers.
- Take it slowly! Whatever you do under pressure is designed to protect you and no matter how dysfunctional that behaviour has become, look after yourself and make small steps. Change that is forced through rarely sticks.

Don't forget – there's more information for each tip in **Part 2** of the book and online at **www.sane.works**

'Assumptions are the termites of relationships.'

– Henry Winkler –

Relationships – we are wired to connect. (Photo by DF)

You are wired to connect and attach to others. It's also true that you might feel unsociable some of the time, you may be quite shy and, unless you are very saintly, you are likely to have the occasional dark thought about your fellow human beings. But the fact remains that in order to get on in business you will need to get on with people. You need to work for people, have them work for you, sell to them, purchase from them and, if you are a manager, put simply, you achieve through them. You will also inevitably form bonds with them and the way that you form these bonds will be influenced by your early experiences of care.

Who you are in any social context is determined by the way people relate to you, whether that's upwards, downwards or sideways. So, whether you favour telling, selling or yelling, it's the expression of you in relation to others that's the key determinant of your effectiveness.

Whole schools of thought are related to this area – from simple but effective classifications of management style to in-depth and rather academic studies of the difference between transactional and transformational leadership. There's no escaping it, whilst Sartre might have grumpily commented, 'Hell is other people', without them, you can't do your job.

Having Your Needs Met

The key foundation to all healthy relationships is the ability of the two parties in that relationship to meet each other's needs. We all come to relationships with needs, but these needs don't have to be just physical (for example, the need for shelter and safety). The needs of other people and ourselves are also often psychological (for example, the need to feel emotionally secure in relationships with other people and part of the group, the need to have status, the need to have certainty). The desire to have these needs met pervades almost all social interactions, often on an unconscious level. This last point is really important as psychotherapists believe that unmet emotional needs during the time that we were growing up can cause us to engage in a whole host of behaviours as adults, some of which even appear to defy logic and sense.

Getting your needs met often affects your behaviour, how you feel, even your brain's ability to concentrate and remember things. Therefore, whether they are met or not largely determines how you perform in the workplace. For example, if you don't believe you are respected and 'safe' in a relationship with a manager (that is, safe from some sort of physical or psychological threat, such as being demoted or being belittled), chances are you will feel and behave differently than if you were to feel that your manager respected you, valued you, and was not potentially going to demote or belittle you. It is a safe bet to say that in most instances, you wouldn't perform day to day as well in the former situation as you would in the latter.

Meeting and connecting as autonomous adults is essential. If you feel you are having your emotional and physical needs met, you are able to take on 'higher tasks'. Maslow discussed this concept of higher tasks in terms of a person striving for 'self-actualisation'. That is, the person who feels safe, who feels valued, who is connected to others can then use all of their strengths to 'be all they can be'.

Relating in the here and now, expressing openness and being comfortable with your own vulnerabilities affects your ability to thrive both professionally and personally. Without your needs being met, you don't have the kind of esteem, cognitive abilities or sense of safety that allows you to explore the environment and cope with change. This kind of exploration of the environment (also known as an 'approach response') has its roots a very long way back in your history, when you were a small child beginning to explore your world. As an adult, it often involves taking the kinds of risks that lead to acquisition of knowledge, skills and experience.

We explored who you are and how you adapt to pressure in the last two chapters. We now turn our attention to the dynamics of how you connect with others. Our starting point is neurology. From there we move on to a description of the fundamentals of interpersonal relationships and an exploration of strokes and transactions; we talk about why all relationships are not just features of the here and now; we explore attachment, intimacy, authenticity and psychological games. Finally, we finish up with three useful techniques borrowed from therapy that help unblock relationship problems.

The Connected Brain and the SCARF

The interest in neuroscience has grown exponentially over the last decade or so. It has become almost commonplace to pop someone in a scanner, ask him or her to solve a problem or have some kind of mental experience and watch parts of the person's brain light up. The results have been incredible and have shed considerable light on how we think and why we act the way we do. They have also shown that we are not quite as sophisticated as we might like to believe and that a lot of our wiring was laid down a long time back in evolutionary history.

The brain is a complex organ that consumes what seems a disproportionate amount of your body's energy – up to a fifth in fact. Even within the brain the total energy requirement is dominated by the neocortex; the most recent and advanced part of the brain in evolutionary terms, and the seat of all of your higher cognitive processes. Damage your neocortex and your whole personality changes.

Nevertheless, your brain has a very simple, overarching organising principle: away from pain and towards pleasure or, put another way, minimising threat and maximising reward.

Recent research has indicated that our psychological needs can be grouped under several different types of domain. Author and consultant David Rock has created a helpful model to explain this. His SCARF model looks at five areas:

- Status.
- Certainty.
- Autonomy.
- Relatedness.
- Fairness.

Rock argues that when you feel your needs in any of these five areas are not being met; your brain codes this as a threat. Looked at the other way: if your needs are met, you will experience a sense of reward.

Let's look at each element in some detail.

Status

This has become a dirty word. Most people are quick to tell you that they are not status conscious, whilst often being just as enthusiastic to tell you about someone they know who emphatically is. The problem is, they are wrong. At the level of our brains, we are all concerned with status. How we talk about status has certainly changed but that doesn't mean that it has gone away as an issue in evolutionary terms.

Our closest animal relatives are the other primates. In primate animal communities, status is closely associated with survival. The high-status animals are healthier and live longer. It's no different with humans. The World Health Organisation's Health Impact Assessment (HIA) is unequivocal: higher income and social status are linked to better health. Returning to the threat-and-reward model, loss of status is recognised at a neurological level as a threat that should be avoided, while increased status is a reward that should be pursued.

Researchers have shown that status is computed in the brain using similar circuits to the one that it uses for numerical processing, so status is seen in relative terms: a way of being 'better' than someone else. This sounds awfully like a crude pecking order but it's subtler than that. Pretty much anything that gives us relative merit activates the same brain circuitry that is associated with reward, and the critical chemical at play here is dopamine, a neurotransmitter that is closely connected with mood.

Of course, the opposite applies to relative loss of status. The brain interprets this as a threat and dopamine levels fall. The cause of loss of status might be as small as being left out of the loop in workplace communications and certainly doesn't need to be as obvious as being overlooked for promotion or as drastic as being made redundant.

Status is not just an individual issue, it applies to groups as well. Organisations are composed of groups and each of these has a collective or social identity and a sense of status in relation to other groups.

You can see this really clearly if you try to make changes to the way people work. If the changes impact on a previously high-status group that stays high status, then this is usually met with little resistance. If the changes impact on a group that stands the chance of an increase in status, then things tend to go smoothly too. The problems really lie with low-status groups that gain nothing from the changes, or even lose status. It's within these groups that trouble brews and resistance can often be found.

All of this begs the question of what to do about status.

Performance Management

First off, we need to be very careful about how we give feedback to other people. It's a crude simplification to say that all feedback is a gift. The neurological evidence is really clear here – feedback that is processed by your brain as being status-reducing will activate the same circuitry as a threat with a big stick!

To make matters worse, most workplace performance management systems are anchored in behaviours, and two groups of people are extremely sensitive to anything that comments on their behaviour. Cast your mind back to Chapter 2, in which we looked at personality behaviour and drivers. If you identified your own drivers as *Please others* or *Be perfect*, any type of behavioural feedback will be very hard to digest and will almost certainly be seen as status-reducing and threatening. Why? Because if you are driven to please others, you are already doing all that you can to make people happy and if you are driven to be perfect, you are already doing all you can to avoid making a mistake.

We aren't suggesting that performance management systems are all abandoned but we do think that they are very capable of doing more harm than good. A relatively untrained manager clutching an appraisal form is about as safe as a learner driver on a motorway! Really good appraiser training is one way to reduce the risk of problems and even better is a clear accent on self-appraisal.

Self-appraisal is a way of dealing with fear of failure when compared with others. Comparisons with colleagues can easily end up with you feeling bad about yourself. This can inhibit creativity and often completely halt action. It's much better to make comparisons with yourself. Done well, this can result in a relentless desire for higher and higher standards and the attaining of a personal best. Think of Steve Jobs, the founder of Apple, for example. He was a perfectionist. It could be argued that his perfectionism had little to do with fear and everything to do with design and aesthetics. If you can increase your sense of status by continually bettering your own performance, all of the evidence points to this being positive, rewarding and sustainable.

Certainty

The brain is a pattern detection and uncertainty reduction system. Uncertainty bothers your neocortex and it fires off the threat response, which takes up energy. The result is that your mind will do what it can to maximise predictability and conserve resources. The more problems that your brain can solve in a relatively automated way, in evolutionary terms at least – the better your long-term survival prospects. Chemically, uncertainty depresses dopamine levels and the reward of certainty increases them.

Try as you might to put your concerns aside, during times of change at work, part of your brain will be dealing with the threat of not knowing. If you are a manager, some of your job will be to deal with the consequences of change. Your role is uncertainty reduction; communicating as clearly as you can about what's happening now, what's going to happen next and what the desired end state is. If you don't do this, people become uncertain and agitated and their output falls dramatically.

Autonomy

This is all about choice. There's a nice idea from cybernetics stating that in order to deal properly with the diversity of problems the world throws at you, you need to have a repertoire of responses which is (at least) as nuanced as the problems you face. This is the principle of requisite variety and is central to pretty much every branch of psychotherapy. The goal of therapists is often to help their clients experience flexible and adaptive responses to the world rather than being stuck in rigid thinking patterns.

Lack of autonomy leads to depressed mood, poor health and even the risk of early death. The now-famous Whitehall study that began in the 1960s looked at the health outcomes of thousands of civil servants over many years. The results were clear – those in lower grades and with less choice about how they conducted their work suffered much greater levels of cardiovascular disease, well beyond what could be explained by other lifestyle factors such as weight and smoking. Lack of autonomy is highly threatening and sustained levels of threat can damage you.

Staying sane means finding a job that gives you some choice about how you work and, if you are a manager, providing as much of that choice as possible. Whether it's having some freedom over your working environment and hours or having access to a coach who can help you puzzle out what the options are when you feel stuck, there's much that we can all do to make workplaces more rewarding and less threatening.

Relatedness

This is fundamentally about deciding whether or not someone is in your tribe. Despite those Athena posters from the 1970s encouraging us to think that 'a stranger is a friend you haven't met', that's not quite the way your brain sees it. For the most part, people you don't know are processed as threats until you learn otherwise. It's true that you have a psychological hunger to connect with others, but at a neurological level, you remain wary. You need to be sure that other people are 'safe'. Perhaps this is no surprise when you consider that for the greatest part of evolutionary history, we all spent our time in small groups of familiar people.

When you feel connected to other people, the level of another neurotransmitter in your brain rises. This hormone is oxytocin and it seems to play a part in both sexual behaviour and parental bonding. Physical contact, from a handshake to a hug, increases oxytocin levels and helps bonding happen.

The implications for this at work are clear. If you want to be at your best, then you need to feel secure, happy and connected. If your boss thinks the stick is more effective than the carrot, or than a friendly relationship with you, he or she is sadly mistaken. If your style as a leader is to exercise power, position and influence through aggression, take note. The positive effects of this style will be extremely short-lived. If you are responsible for organisation design, there is something else that you should take note of as well: people tend to work better in small groups. Gallup, the experts in measuring workplace engagement, has known this for some time. Contained in their Q12 survey is a question that asks whether you have a best friend at work. If you do, your engagement is likely to be much higher than someone who doesn't. And if you don't, then it might be an idea to cultivate one!

Fairness

The last element of Rock's model covers a word that is more commonly used in organisations than any other! We are acutely aware when we are being treated in a less than equitable manner. Unfairness is a threat and anything that we perceive as unjustified treatment to ourselves in relation to others is something that we find very hard to let go of and overlook.

Relationship Fundamentals

Moving on from considering threats and rewards at the level of the brain, it is useful to think about the way in which we relate to others and how this differs from person to person. Back in the late 1950s, an American psychologist called William Schutz created a theory of interpersonal relations that survives to this day. He argued that by using a model with just three dimensions – control, openness and inclusion – we can understand the fundamentals of most human interactions and we can shed significant light on group dynamics.

- **Control** – This is concerned with achieving the right level of control in your relationships; the extent to which you want to be in charge and in control of what's going on or independent, free and less accountable. It's also about how much you experience being controlled and how you feel about that.
- **Openness** – This is all about achieving the right level of disclosure with others, the extent to which you want to be open and expressive, and how much you want this from others.
- **Inclusion** – The third dimension is about achieving the right level of contact with others. It looks at the extent to which you may be and want to be included, recognised and around people, as opposed to being alone and not included. It also considers how much you want to include others.

Schutz's model is called Fundamental Interpersonal Relationships Orientation or FIRO. It's a neat model in that it allows you to explore differences in a transparent and non-judgemental way. If you, for example, have a low need for inclusion and on the whole you are not included, you will be seen as an independent person and perhaps something of a loner. Of course, you could be quite happy that way and you would find it stressful if people tried to bring you into the fold too much. On the other hand, if your need for control is low and you have a low need to control others, your self-image might be of a rebel, someone who fits less comfortably into organisations and who might be happier working on the outside as an associate or consultant. You might remember the idea of openness from the OCEAN model when we looked at personality. Suffice to say, in the context of relationships at work, some people have a high need for openness and some people have a low one.

Strokes and Transactions

Relationships need constant attention and feeding if they are not to wither and die. Originally a term created in Transactional Analysis, the stroke is a unit of recognition, so called because the first way in which you were recognised as an infant was through touch, but clearly it's just as applicable to showing your love for your dog, cat or any other pet!

A stroke can be anything that shows you acknowledge the presence of another person: a smile, a joke, a hug or a handshake. But a stroke doesn't need to be a positive experience. Even a harsh word, a frown or a punch is a form of recognition. In this sense, Oscar Wilde was right when he said, 'There is only one thing in the world worse than being talked about, and that's not being talked about'.

We all have relational needs. Some of these were satisfied in childhood and some weren't. If you had a good enough upbringing, you are more likely than not to engage in open, honest, loving and mutually appreciative relationships with other people. If, however, some or all of your relational needs were not met when you were little, you will have learnt other ways to get attention and recognition. These ways are not wrong or manipulative, as they were designed to get you what was needed at the time – no matter how dysfunctional they might look to others, or indeed to you as an adult.

We tend to be aware of unmet relational needs when we say that someone is attention-seeking but invitations to give strokes are not always that obvious. Sometimes, the methods that people employ are too subtle to spot and sometimes we are strangers to ourselves. This is not surprising as the origins of so much of our behaviour lie outside conscious awareness.

Parent, Adult, Child

One way of thinking about how you relate to others is to consider that you exist in three different states, three different patterns of thoughts, feelings and behaviours. These have been called a number of names by psychologists and psychotherapists over the years but the simplest is to call them Parent, Adult and Child. This is the PAC model from Transactional Analysis.

- **Parent** – The Parent part of you is the store of all the material that you took on board as you were growing up in the company of bigger people – parents or similar figures. This is like a reservoir of borrowed material that can be added to as your life progresses and you come into contact with other authority figures. Another way you could think about the Parent is as a set of computer programs. These programs tend to run outside your conscious awareness, you could say offline if you want to continue with the IT metaphor. Some of these programs have been passed down the generations with minimal re-coding. Many of them have been essential to keeping you safe in the world. But some programs are like their real-life computer equivalents in that they contain bugs. A lot of therapy is about recognising when you have become dominated by this state and where you have taken on board psychological material that isn't yours. Either way, whenever you think, feel or act in a way that has been unconsciously borrowed from a parent or parent figure, we can say that you are in the Parent state.

- **Adult** – This part of you is all about conscious awareness of what is happening in the present moment. When you are in this state you are integrating all of your experience, thoughts and feelings from the past and you are making sense of what is happening in the here and now. You might be reflecting on what you have been taught and what your values are and could well be feeling emotions but what you are thinking and feeling belongs to the here and now and not to the past. If you are in Adult mode you are likely to feel sad if you hear of the death of a friend but your sadness belongs to the present and is a proportionate reaction to something that is genuinely upsetting. What you won't do when you are in this state is act on your feelings without reflection and you won't be hijacked by your emotions either. You could see the Adult as integrating everything that makes you who you are; a part of you that is in control, like a pilot flying a plane.

- **Child** – This is the part of you associated with the thoughts, feelings and behaviours that were encoded in your past. These are your past experiences and their memory traces can be activated at any time. Faced with an aggressive and domineering boss, who finds continual fault with what you do, you may complain to a friend that this boss makes you feel 'small'. Feeling small can also be the same as feeling vulnerable or not-OK. If this boss reminds you at some level of a critical parent, the way that you deal with him or her may be as much about the past as it is about the present.

Pretty much everything that is historic is stored in the Parent or Child states. The greater the emotion associated with past experience, the firmer this storage will be and this can cause you to be locked into patterns of behaviour that are rigidly maintained and compulsively repeated.

The State You're In

Knowing when you are in Parent, Adult or Child state is an essential part of self-awareness and staying sane. If you talk with a coach who has a psychodynamic way of working, or with a therapist, you will be encouraged to reflect on the way that you are thinking, feeling and acting. Some therapists even use words like 'decontamination' to talk about helping you free yourself from Parental material that you have imported, taken to be yours and which now restricts the choices that you feel you have.

We contain within ourselves mini versions of what we once were. (Photo by CW)

You can work out if you are in Parent, Adult or Child state by using the following:

- **Pay attention to your behaviour** – What are you doing right now? How does your body feel? If you are looking up from under your fringe, hopping on one foot like a child needing the loo (aka the 'wee dance' for those of you who have had experience with toddlers) or kicking and screaming in an adult version of the terrible twos, the chances are that you are in a Child state. If, on the other hand you are handing down a lecture, standing with your hands on hips pointing in an accusing manner, you are likely to be in a Parent state. You could, by the way, be rushing to soothe someone who has become upset, which is equally parental.

- **Think about how you are interacting with someone** – Does the interaction make you feel big or small? What is being said? What is the other person doing? There's a big difference between the response, 'Time you got a watch' when you ask for the time from someone and a factual reply that it's nearly three o'clock! Some therapists call the pattern of our interactions with others transactions; hence transactional analysis. If you are having a conversation with a colleague and you are feeling distinctly like a child, the chances are that they are behaving like a parent. Incidentally, we are all very good at listening beyond the words and the meaning that we extract from any interaction is always at the psychological level. The words are less important than the tone and the tone is less important than the body language when we register any disconnect between the three. Regardless of exactly what has been said, we are acutely aware if we are being talked down to or patronised.

- **Reflect on your history** – If you are aware of a feeling, it can be very helpful to ask yourself how old you are feeling right now and whether you can recall having a feeling like this in your personal history. This can give you a direct line of sight to the possible reliving of something from your past. Asking these questions to our clients during coaching or therapy, we have often been struck by how powerful tracing back a strong feeling can be.

Getting Close to People

If one of your primary needs is to form relationships with other people at work or outside work, how do you do this? Psychotherapy has a lot to say here that sheds light on how we are with each other.

How you form bonds with other people developed in your early life and was reinforced throughout your childhood. Therefore the way you think about other people, what you expect them to do in relationships, what you want from relationships, what typical relationships should look like, were all formed a long time before you entered work!

As we all learned in pre-school, how we behave determines to a substantial extent how other people behave back. If you are caring towards others, they tend to be caring towards you. If you are 'cold' emotionally towards others, demonstrating little warmth or affection, they tend to be the same towards you. So, if you have a blueprint that says

'I am OK on my own, I don't need to be close to others', then it is fairly easy to see how that would influence you to behave in a way similar to that discussed in the example. This would then be more likely to elicit similar behaviour from others, which will serve as evidence to reinforce the belief that 'I don't need to be close to others'. Therefore, patterns of relating to other people become self-reinforcing over time. This makes them difficult to break. However, patterns of attachment can be changed; we are never immune to the influence of new experiences. With time and the repeated occurrence of new, more positive experiences with other people, unhelpful patterns of attachment can gradually begin to change.

Whilst patterns of attachment vary from person to person, they vary in ways that can be loosely categorised for adults into four main types.

- **Secure** – People with a secure attachment often find it easy to form close emotional bonds with others and will be content in mutually supportive relationships where each person depends on the other, especially in times of difficulty or stress. They are also confident in their ability to act as an independent adult in the world, and in their own self-worth as a person. They will be able to take criticism and contain the distress it causes. Secure attachment has its origins in being well cared for as a child. As grown-ups we exist in the world with the view: I'm OK, and other people are OK.

- **Insecure, anxious-preoccupied** – People with this type of attachment often want to be very emotionally close to others and are at risk of excessive worrying and displaying unhelpfully high levels of emotion in their behaviour. They often find that their high demands for emotional closeness are rejected by others. This perceived lack of emotional closeness runs the risk of developing into dependency, as they often see themselves as being at fault for the lack of emotional responsiveness they seek from their partners. This leads to feelings of discomfort and self-doubt as the person believes themselves to have low worth in the eyes of others. In short: others are OK, but I'm not.

- **Dismissive-avoidant** – People with this type of attachment tend to be most comfortable when not in emotionally close relationships. This shows itself as a willingness to be very independent, with the person often behaving in a way that demonstrates no obvious need for emotional close attachments to others. The risk of this attachment style is that the person does not have much insight into the emotional experiences of themselves or others, and can view interpersonal situations in a cold, thought-dominated way. As such, they do not recognise the emotional aspects of events, and often manage criticisms, disapproval or perceived rejection with avoidance (for example, they may avoid or become more detached from a manager who provides them with constructive feedback, rather than reflecting on and managing any difficult emotions this feedback causes). It can be best summarised as an attachment style where the person believes: 'I'm OK, you're not OK'.

- **Fearful-avoidant** – People with this attachment style often want close emotional relationships, but also find those relationships threatening and/or uncomfortable. This is because they find it difficult to establish trusting mutual relationships. As you may be able to tell, this attachment style can promote contradictory beliefs and emotions about relationships, leaving the person confused as they both desire and don't desire close relationships. They often have low self-worth. They may see others as being unworthy of trust and likely to hurt them emotionally in some way. As a result, they may not emotionally express their needs. However, they will also find it very challenging to reflect on and manage their own emotional distress. In summary, this attachment style can be described with the statement: 'I'm not OK, you're not OK'.

These attachment patterns play out at work as much as in your personal life.

How We Structure Time Together

Given that we all desire some kind of connection with others and that we are predisposed to form bonds in different ways, it's interesting to explore how we actually go about it on a day-to-day basis.

Time is a vacuum that we fill with our behaviour. (Photo by CW)

Even if you have a very stable pattern of attachment and if your interactions with others at work are for the most part adult to adult in nature, it doesn't necessarily follow that open, intimate and mutually supportive relationships will always be what you engage in. Instead, you might find yourself involved in other types of interaction.

- **Rituals** – Fairly superficial interactions made up of stylised elements in which you might ask, 'Are you OK?' and the response could be, 'Mustn't grumble'. No information has really been exchanged, few feelings have been experienced, but it's at least recognition of each other's existence.

- **Pastimes** – Interchanges that are less ritualised but still have a recognisable pattern and structure. You might imagine two young men standing side by side looking at a car and talking about its features and their views on the make of car in general. They might be taking it in turns to comment, to engage in banter or to do impressions of a favourite TV presenter. There are some brilliant observations of this nature in Kate Fox's delightful book *Watching the English*. Without the exchange of much personal information, these types of interactions are nevertheless experienced as effective ways of coming alongside other people and getting to know them.

- **Activities** – Explicitly about something where there is a shared and agreed joint outcome, this might be a project at work or being part of a sports team. It's here that your interactions are in the service of something, and the sense of this common aim is what creates the feeling of connection.

- **Psychological games** – Characterised by repetitive patterns of negative behaviour that we seem to set up for ourselves without our awareness, they only lead us to conclude, 'Here I go again ...' or 'Why does this keep happening to me?'

A Bit More About Psychological Games

Psychological games are much more emotionally charged than rituals, pastimes and activities. These games involve drama in which you take a position that shifts during the course of the game and the end result is that you usually feel worse rather than better for having taken part. In the late 1960s, Stephen Karpman pointed out that dramatic inter-changes involve a triangular pattern of three positions – persecutor, rescuer and victim.

A typical game at work might be where someone invites you to give him or her some advice. The game starts with you believing that you can really help, but the more you try to offer solutions to the person's issues, the more you seem to get rebuffed. Eventually you become irritated and either walk away or say something sharp and critical to the other person and then regret it.

This is the game that was called *Why Don't You? ... Yes, But* by Eric Berne. What's happening in the game is that the person apparently asking for help isn't really asking for help as a grown-up at all. What they are doing is luring you into a game where they can explore the feelings of not-OK-ness which they first experienced as a child. What your fellow game-player is looking for is sympathy and the best place to get this is as a victim who is either going to be rescued or persecuted.

Over the years, psychotherapists have identified numerous games and a complete list is well beyond the scope of this book. If, however, you find that some of your relationships at work have a distinctly gamey feel about them, there are things that you can do.

- **What's going on?** – Firstly step back and survey what's going on. Ask yourself in detail what's happening over and over again?
- **How does it start?** – Next try to work out how the game starts.
- **What's the sequence?** – Then go through the game step by step and piece together what sequence it follows.
- **Where does it end?** – Ask yourself how the game ends and how you usually feel.

Building up your awareness of game-playing can help you avoid get-ting sucked in. Ultimately, what you have to be prepared to do is step outside the drama triangle and see it for what it is.

Other Complications

Modern working practices are often not conducive to the forming and maintenance of relationships. We seem to live in a hurried and transactional age in which a premium is placed on speed. We are also physically remote from each other a lot of the time and overly dependent on text-based methods of maintaining connection. It can take a special effort to make your organisational culture a truly human experience.

Here are some of the challenges that we see as coaches and therapists.

- **Productivity demands** – There's the continual myth that we are more productive when we do several things at once. There's absolutely no basis for this. In 2005, the BBC reported on a research study, funded by Hewlett-Packard and conducted by the Institute of Psychiatry at the University of London, that found, 'Workers distracted by email and phone calls suffer a fall in IQ more than twice that found in marijuana smokers.' The psychologist who led the study called this new 'infomania' a serious threat to workplace productivity. Trying to maintain relationships with other people whilst juggling smartphones, email and social media is a recipe for a degraded interpersonal experience.

- **Acceptable behaviours** – Despite the prevalence of competency frameworks that encourage us to consider how work is carried out as much as the end result, we tolerate some remarkably rude behaviours in the 21st-century office. How often have you sat in meetings with people who are clearly suffering from what Linda Stone, writing in the Harvard Business Review in 2007 called 'continuous partial attention'? They fiddle under the table with their smart phones and are rarely fully present in the room. The ubiquitous teleconference makes matters worse. For a wonderfully light-hearted take on the latter, have a look at Trip and Tyler's 'A Conference Call in Real Life' on YouTube.

- **Structures** – Whilst we aren't advocating a return to command-and-control bureaucracies in which change proceeded at glacial pace, we now seem to have the opposite problem: many people in organisations not being entirely clear what is expected of them and yet having to operate at a considerable pace. Just as your organisation completes one restructure then the next one starts. Not only do relationships suffer as a result of role ambiguity but a lot of tacit knowledge is lost in the process.

- **Social status** – In the words of the wonderful Alain de Botton in *Status Anxiety*:

  People who hold important positions in society are commonly labelled 'somebodies' and their inverse 'nobodies' – both of which are, of course, nonsensical descriptors, for we are all, by necessity, individuals with distinct identities and comparable claims on existence. Such words are nevertheless an apt vehicle for conveying the disparate treatment accorded to different groups. Those without status are all but invisible: they are treated brusquely by others, their complexities trampled upon and their singularities ignored.

- **Technology** – We have already said enough about that one... if we say anything else you will get distracted and start fiddling with your phone!

- **Leadership style** – This one will never go away. It's easier to form relationships with some bosses than others and the impact of their style on the morale of their teams should never be underestimated. Management writers have been talking about the long shadow that leaders cast for many years.

Whatever style you have as a boss, or you respond to in those who lead you, it will have a relationship component. Of all the tasks of leadership, it's the job of inspiring other people that has the biggest emotional component. In the words of Pendleton and Furnham in *Leadership – All You Need to Know*, 'The leader has to connect with the feelings of the workforce and be able to appeal to those feelings if people are to become motivated and to buy into change. Inspiration demands passion as well as thought in order to win hearts and minds'.

Another way of looking at leadership style is provided by management consultants Hay Group. In their taxonomy, it's not hard to spot the styles that allow relationships to flourish and those where forging human bonds would be much more of a challenge.

Leadership Style

Style	This looks like...
Coercive *'Just do it the way I tell you to.'*	Lots of directives and control. Plenty of negative and corrective feedback. The expectation of immediate compliance.
Authoritative *'Let me tell you where we are going as a team.'*	The articulation of a clear vision and direction. Selling of this vision and the solicitation of feedback. An accent on persuasion and a clear focus on standards.
Affiliative *'People first, task second.'*	The promotion of friendly interactions. Not so much attention on task directions, goals and standards. Identification of opportunities for positive feedback.
Democratic *'Let's decide together.'*	Careful listening. Decisions by consensus. More accent on the reward of team performance than on individual contribution.
Pacesetting *'If you can't do it right, I'll do it myself.'*	Leading from the front by modelling what's needed. Little sympathy for poor performance. Detailed instructions but not much focus on rectifying underperformance. Quick removal of responsibility if high levels of performance are not forthcoming.
Coaching *'What did you learn? What would you do differently? What can we improve upon?'*	Helping people find their unique strengths. The encouragement of learning and setting of development goals. Feedback and lots of open questions rather than direction.

Source: Managerial Style Workbook, Hay Group 2009

None of these styles is entirely right or entirely wrong. Some are better than others at certain times and some will appeal to you personally whilst others won't. But one thing is for sure, leadership style is very rarely neutral!

Really Toxic Bosses and Colleagues

The fact is they do exist and at some stage you are likely to end up working for one or with one. Quite apart from the simple risk of overdone strengths in anyone, you might be unfortunate enough to be working with someone who has an extreme personality. Oliver James talks about this in great detail in his book *Office Politics: How to Thrive in a World of Lying, Backstabbing and Dirty Tricks*.

Part of our work as business psychologists is to try to look beyond superficial charm and well-rehearsed answers and identify the characteristics in candidates that they would rather we didn't know. Our top three risky characters, and ones that we are quite sure you'd be better off not working for or with, are the psychopath, the narcissist and the hubristic leader. We often run seminars on this topic and we sometimes wonder who is in the audience!

All of these personality classifications are, of course, at the extreme. The problem is, they are over-represented in senior management circles. People who get to the top in organisations are by definition abnormal because most people don't.

The Psychopath

This is not the Hannibal Lecter character from *Silence of the Lambs* – Hollywood has done a lot to distort what this extreme personality is all about, but then you'd expect that since they are trying to sell entertainment. Being an organisational psychopath isn't about blood, guts and murder. It's often less colourful, but much more destructive on a bigger scale. Organisations that have been led by psychopaths have crashed and burned. Think WorldCom, Enron and Arthur Anderson to name but three.

And before you think of it as a rare phenomenon, you should be aware that 1% of the UK population is a psychopath and that means over 600,000 people!

So what is a psychopath? The best place to start is the lengthy tome that is the *Diagnostic and Statistical Manual of Mental Disorders* (DSM-5). If you don't happen to have a copy lying around, let us enlighten you. Here's a description used by US psychiatrists (psychopathology is defined as Antisocial Personality Disorder in the US):

Antisocial Personality Disorder – A pervasive pattern of disregard for and violation of the rights of others, occurring since age 15 years, as indicated by three (or more) of the following:

1. Failure to conform to social norms with respect to lawful behaviours, as indicated by repeatedly performing acts that are grounds for unrest.
2. Deceitfulness as indicated by repeated lying, use of aliases, or conning others for personal profit or pleasure.
3. Impulsivity or failure to plan ahead.
4. Irritability and aggressiveness, as indicated by repeated physical fights or assaults.
5. Reckless disregard for the safety of self or others.
6. Consistent irresponsibility, as indicated by repeated failure to sustain consistent work behaviour or honour financial obligations.
7. Lack of remorse, as indicated by being indifferent to or rationalising having hurt, mistreated or stolen from another.

Source: DSM-5, Cluster B Personality Disorders 301.7

It's the last point that is particularly telling as an identifier. The true psychopath feels no guilt at their actions – no matter how much they have lied and cheated. They feel empathy for their victims but that empathy is cold. They are acutely tuned into the emotions of others but they are not in the least moved by them. Others are just pawns in their game and are completely expendable. Often very charming and socially skilled, corporate psychopaths make very dangerous bosses indeed.

Are any of these behaviours familiar?

- Publicly humiliating people, having temper tantrums and ridiculing others.
- Making promises that cannot possibly be kept and then putting the responsibility solely onto someone else.
- Malicious spreading of lies.
- Excessive pushing of their personal agenda.
- Emotions that seem to change like traffic lights.
- Intentionally isolating people or resources.
- Rapid blaming of other people even though he or she is the guilty party.
- Encouraging peers or subordinates to harass or humiliate each other.
- Taking credit where none is due.
- Stealing ideas or property.
- Making threats – veiled or otherwise.
- Management exclusively by bilateral arrangements – little group decision-making.
- Invading of the privacy of others.
- Having multiple sexual partners at work.
- Will do 'whatever it takes' to win business.

Of course, not everything a psychopath does is bad. In an excellent and entertaining book, *The Wisdom of Psychopaths*, Kevin Dutton points out that:

Psychopaths are assertive. Psychopaths don't procrastinate. Psychopaths tend to focus on the positive. Psychopaths don't take things personally; they don't beat themselves up if things go wrong, even if they're to blame. And they're pretty cool under pressure. Those kinds of characteristics aren't just important in the business arena, but also in everyday life.

Small wonder, then, that they continue to thrive.

That's what the psychopath looks like on the outside. What might be happening on the inside? It's thought that this personality develops as a result of failures in attachment and attunement at a time when the brain is at its most plastic – the pre-verbal infant. Put simply, the psychopath has probably experienced little love as a child or very inconsistent care at least. They have grown up with a strong expectation of being abandoned and they learnt to get their emotional needs met through manipulation.

If you suspect that you are working for a psychopath, the best advice is to get out and put as much distance between you and them as possible. If this isn't an option, Oliver James makes some sensible suggestions, which are similar to the ones that Paul Babiak and world psychopath expert Robert Hare make in *Snakes in Suits – When Psychopaths go to Work*.

- **Don't accept their psychological rubbish** – In public it's wise to let them think they have won but do not internalise the unhappiness that they project onto you. This is exceptionally difficult and there will be times when you are convinced that it is you who is in the wrong but, as James points out, the psychopath is dumping psychological rubbish onto you. Whatever you do, do not accept it as being yours.

- **Assume that everything they are telling you is a lie** – Absolute masters at charm and manipulation, the way they come across can be utterly compelling. See it for what it probably is – just an act.

- **Check out what they are saying about you with other people** – Claude Steiner put this beautifully when he stated that alienation = oppression + mystification. A psychopathic boss or colleague is highly manipulative and they aren't in the least bit concerned about who they lie to and what they lie about as long as they don't get caught and they get their needs met. They rely on isolating you from others and confusing you. You must maintain contact with people, stay abreast of the facts and feel like you are taking action to look after yourself.

The Narcissist

Not quite as damaging but still highly toxic is the narcissistic boss or colleague. Working for or in close proximity to a narcissist is like having a vampire bat on your neck, sucking you dry. What the narcissist needs more than anything else is a ready supply of adoration, adulation, admiration and approval. If you can do this, you have a use. If you run dry, you will be quickly discarded in favour of someone else who can!

Turning again to DSM-5, Narcissistic Personality Disorder is described as a pervasive pattern of grandiosity (in fantasy or behaviour), need for admiration and lack of empathy, visible by early adulthood and present in a variety of contexts, as indicated by five (or more) of the following characteristics.

- **A grandiose sense of self-importance** – The narcissist exaggerates achievements and talents, and expects to be recognised as superior without commensurate achievements.

- **A pre-occupation with fantasies of unlimited success** – These may be associated with power, brilliance, beauty or ideal love.

- **Belief that he or she is special and unique** – As a result, they can only be understood by, or should associate with, other special or high-status people (or institutions).

- **A need for excessive admiration** – From everyone around them.

- **A sense of entitlement** – Including unreasonable expectations of especially favourable treatment or automatic compliance with his or her expectations.

- **Being interpersonally exploitative** – Taking advantage of others to achieve his or her own ends.

- **Lacking empathy** – And being unwilling to recognise or identify with the feelings or needs of others.
- **Envious** – Frequently envious of others or believing that others are envious of him or her.
- **Arrogant** – Displaying arrogant, haughty behaviours or attitudes.

DSM-5, Cluster B Personality Disorders 301.81

The origin of narcissism is also thought to lie early on, developmentally. Psychotherapists argue that we are all narcissistic to begin with. As tiny infants, we really are the centre of our own worlds but, of course, there comes a time when we need to begin the process of separating from our caregivers and becoming an individual in our own right. This is a traumatic event for all of us but eventually most of us find our way through it.

We talked about attachment earlier and in stable attachment we understand that our caregivers will not always be available but that we are fundamentally safe, they continue to exist and love us even when we can't see them and that they return to us. We start to develop the belief that we exist alongside other people and that they have rights and feelings that should be respected. Narcissists, on the other hand, seem to be trapped in perpetual early childhood, terrified that unless they are 'special' and not ordinary like the rest of us, they will be abandoned and abandonment will lead to death. Some therapists believe that there is a connection here with over-protective, intrusive and smothering parenting styles. The answer to the narcissist's fear is to create a false persona, a special, gifted or wonderful being – a special child who runs less risk of ceasing to exist. Underneath the false self exists a very frightened small person.

If you are working for or with a narcissist, the same applies as to the psychopath. Really, the best thing you can do is remove yourself from the situation but there are other alternatives.

- **Define very clearly what you want (if anything) from a relationship with them** – Remember, you are just a mirror in which they can admire themselves, a source of narcissistic supply, which allows them to maintain their false self.

- **Keep a clear sense of who you are** – Build your self-worth outside of the relationship that you have with them.
- **Try very hard not to prick their bubble** – The narcissist's greatest fear is the sudden collapse of their false self and having to confront the true self beneath. This fear can provoke an extreme reaction to anyone who threatens him or her.
- **Dig deep for compassion** – Recognise the misery of their condition and do not leap to the conclusion that their apparent self-love is genuine. Narcissism has not been called malignant self-love without reason. It's highly likely that what caused them to be the way they are is the pattern of care that they experienced as a small child.
- **Listen to them** – On a day-to-day basis, find a way of agreeing with them, but don't expect to please them. Try to persuade them that what you need is what they need.

The Hubrist

A definition of hubris is extreme pride or arrogance. Hubris often indicates a loss of contact with reality, disregard for others and an overestimation of one's own competence or capabilities.

Whilst this may sound like the psychopath or the narcissist, there's an argument that a hubristic boss or colleague is behaving this way not because of some deep problem but as a result of being exposed to a culture in which he or she has too much power and that this power is allowed to be exercised unchecked. As such, what they develop is an acquired personality disorder.

Recognising this, the Daedalus Trust (www.daedalustrust.com) was set up to help 'rein in reckless leaders', arguing that:

> *Over-confident CEOs who overpay for acquisitions, fund managers who overstep the bounds of their mandate, public sector*

managers or politicians who ignore the limits of legality – it seems power corrupts many people who exercise it.

The work of the trust is to shed light on what happens to otherwise normal people when exercising power distorts their thinking and changes their personality. The end point is the type of governance in organisations that prevents leaders riding roughshod over employees and shareholders. If it doesn't feel like this type of governance yet exists in your organisation, you could do worse than following the recommendations in relation to psychopaths and narcissists above.

Repair Work

So given all that we have discussed, what should you do if you find yourself in a relationship at work that is stuck and damaging but perhaps not downright toxic? Relationships can go wrong and often need some remedial activity to bring them back on track if they are not to unravel completely. This is a convenient point to re-visit Martha.

Martha Undertaking Repair Work

Remember, Martha is well qualified, she has a lot of experience and she's had feedback from peers and her team that she knows her stuff and she's making results happen.

In the second coaching session, Martha talked about her relationship with her line manager, the R&D director. The problem is that every encounter with her boss left her feeling deflated and demoralised and quite seriously questioning the contribution that she was making.

Martha felt that her boss favoured other people over her and that she was constantly under threat of being criticised by him. To make matters worse, Martha's boss was inconsistent. Some days he was as nice as pie and came into her office with a laugh and a joke and then – without warning and often in public – he was on her case with harsh and disproportionate severity.

Things had come to a head recently as Martha was working on a high-profile project, the outcome of which was really important to the future of her department. Her boss was sponsoring this project and if she could land it, in theory it could be a route to recognition and promotion for her. It's just a shame that she dreaded progress review meetings and, even though the project was going well, she couldn't believe that her boss was happy with her.

Martha's coach asked some questions to get a few more details. Together they concluded that her boss was in most ways a normal person and certainly didn't seem to have an extreme or dangerous personality. It seemed more of an inter-personal problem: something that arose between Martha and her boss and that wasn't necessarily a feature of other relationships that her boss had at work.

Given all that we have explored, if you were Martha's coach, what would you make of this?

- If you apply the SCARF model, it's clear that she perceives her boss as a threat. Her status is under attack and she's on the defensive. It's also true that her boss is spooking her because he's inconsistent, that she feels her freedom to act is constrained, that try as she might she can't seem to connect with him and that other people are having an easier time than she is.

- Taking a FIRO perspective, you also recognise that her boss has a much higher need for control than Martha has a desire to be controlled and, in truth, neither of them is that open with their feelings.

- Looking through the lens of the PAC model makes you realise that for the most part Martha feels like a child in the presence of her boss and that he has a nasty habit of snagging a feeling that Martha had when she was growing up with an older sibling who seemed to take great delight in bullying and humiliating her and with whom she finds it difficult to get on with even now.

- Furthermore, in the coaching session, when she reflected on the way in which she was brought up, Martha realised that as the youngest child of older parents her role was to fit in and conform to the needs of others and that any expression of vulnerability was discouraged. As an adult, she tends to think her way out of problems and she is suspicious of any strong emotions she feels. Some people have called poor Martha a bit of a 'cold fish'!

- Lastly, although Martha gets on well with people in her organisation and she is a popular member of her team, she doesn't really have a best friend at work and most of her interactions with her colleagues are characterised by light banter. When she feels aggrieved she tends not to vocalise it, preferring instead to go home and ruminate on why things aren't working out.

Having done a bit of diagnosis, the question is what to do about Martha's relationship. The following three ideas from the world of therapy might prove useful.

Step 1 – Action-Feeling Statements

The first thing you can do in relationship repair work is to bring the relationship issue firmly into the here and now. One very simple way to keep the conversation adult to adult and free of a defensive or critical overtone is to simply say what you are feeling. You need to do this without interpretation or blame so it wouldn't work to say to Martha's boss that 'You make me angry', for example.

Our major emotions are sadness, anger, fear and joy and simply stating them can be exceptionally powerful. If you keep the focus on the emotion and not on the people involved, it's surprising how this can cut through to the heart of what's happening.

Martha might say to her boss: 'When I am publicly criticised it makes me very sad'. In this way she is clearly stating her feelings and linking them to a specific event. Stating her feelings and then remaining silent can be incredibly disarming. In the coaching session, Martha discussed how she tended to gabble and then try to justify herself when she was upset.

Step 2 – Perceptual Positions

Another technique, this time from the world of Gestalt therapy, is to take two chairs and in turn sit on each whilst fully occupying the world of the person whose position you are taking.

If we did this, we'd ask Martha to sit on the first chair as herself. We'd ask her to face her boss in the empty second chair and state her case in its entirety.

Next, we'd invite her to stand up, walk over to the second chair and repeat the exercise from her boss's point of view. We would ask her to try and sit like her boss, talk like him and use his turn of phrase to describe what he sees, thinks, feels and experiences as he looks at Martha. We'd say to Martha that she should do this in the first person just as if her boss was occupying her body.

Then we'd invite Martha to stand up and occupy a neutral third position as if she was a fly on the wall. We'd ask her to describe what she could see, hear and feel to be happening between these two people.

Finally, we'd say to Martha that she should return to the first chair that she occupied and see if the world looks and feels any different. The chances are, it would.

Step 3 – Relationship Checklist

Let's imagine you find yourself in a similar position to Martha. You are in a workplace relationship that isn't working. Nothing dramatic is happening, your boss isn't psychopathic or narcissistic and you don't end up in floods of tears every time you have an encounter. It's not even as if you see the world in very different ways but somehow you don't quite get on. Is there a process that might help?

Family therapist Virginia Satir came up with a clever set of steps that she called The Daily Temperature Reading. Whilst these might feel a bit odd at first, with careful application, they can make a real difference.

- **Appreciations** – Start off by listing a number of things that you really appreciate about the other person. In British culture, this probably needs to be done without too much gushing and with a bit of subtlety but, as Satir points out, it's a vital step in building up the emotional credit bank. You might, for example, say to your boss that you really admire how she cuts through complexity and has the courage to state things as she sees them.

- **Wishes, hopes and dreams** – Next, tell the other person about what you are really hoping for. This needs to done in the context of what you are doing in your job and shouldn't be too abstract. You might tell your boss that you are really looking forward to the final project board meeting and you are hoping that the CEO is going to be delighted with how the project has been delivered as you have so much good news to tell.

- **New information** – This is the point where you talk about what the other person isn't yet aware of. One of our clients who had a rather curmudgeonly boss got into the habit of maintaining a 'reasons to be cheerful' list, which proved a useful resource to draw on when he felt that his boss was becoming negative or suspicious that things weren't going to plan. Clearly, this is all about telling a number of as yet untold good-news stories and it's not about spin or concealment of the truth.

- **Puzzles** – Next, you can clear up big or little mysteries before they become suspicions, false assumptions or big problems. If you do this in the spirit of wondering out loud rather than levelling an accusation, it will work better. You could say to your boss that you wonder why there's always an air of tension around the project when it seems to be hitting all of its milestones.

- **Complaints with request for change** – Lastly, say what you want and not what you don't want. You could say to your boss that you really value her feedback but when she has anything that she's particularly concerned about could she have a pre-meeting with you rather than saving her frustrations for a public forum. In turn you could promise to ensure that she's really well briefed.

The Challenge of Organisational Life and Culture

Martha, like all of us, doesn't work in a vacuum. She works for an organisation that has a particular culture and this culture has an impact on norms of behaviour. Some cultures encourage human relationships and some don't.

Here's a little story, written by Claude Steiner many years ago. It's called 'A Warm Fuzzy Tale'.

Once upon a time, a long time ago, there lived two happy people called Tim and Maggie with their two children, John and Lucy. To understand how happy they were you have to understand how things were in those days.

You see, in those happy days everyone was given a small, soft Fuzzy Bag when born. Any time a person reached into this bag they were able to pull out a Warm Fuzzy. Warm Fuzzies were very much in demand because whenever someone was given a Warm Fuzzy it made them feel warm and fuzzy all over.

In those days it was very easy to get Warm Fuzzies. Anytime that somebody felt like it, he might walk up to you and say, 'I'd like to have a Warm Fuzzy.'

You would then reach into your bag and pull out a Fuzzy the size of a child's hand. As soon as the Fuzzy saw the light of day it would smile and blossom into a large, shaggy, Warm Fuzzy. When you laid the Warm Fuzzy on the person's head, shoulder or lap it would snuggle up and melt right against their skin and make them feel good all over.

People were always asking each other for Warm Fuzzies, and since they were always given freely, getting enough of them was never a problem. There were always plenty to go around, and so everyone was happy and felt warm and fuzzy most of the time.

One day a bad witch who made salves and potions for sick people became angry because everyone was so happy and feeling good and no one was buying potions and salves. The witch was very clever and devised a very wicked plan. One beautiful morning while Maggie was playing with her daughter the witch crept up to Tim and whispered in his ear, 'See here, Tim, look at all the Fuzzies that Maggie is giving to Lucy. You know, if she keeps it up she is going to run out and then there won't be any left for you!'

Tim was astonished. He turned to the witch and asked, 'Do you mean to tell me that there isn't a Warm Fuzzy in our bag every time we reach into it?'

And the witch answered, 'No, absolutely not, and once you run out, that's it. You don't have any more.' With this the witch flew away on a broom, laughing and cackling all the way.

Tim took this to heart and began to notice every time Maggie gave away a Warm Fuzzy. He got very worried because he liked Maggie's Warm Fuzzies very much and did not want to give them up.

He certainly did not think it was right for Maggie to be spending all her Warm Fuzzies on the children and other people.

Tim began to complain or sulk when he saw Maggie giving Warm Fuzzies to somebody else, and because Maggie loved him very much, she stopped giving Warm Fuzzies to other people as often, and reserved most of them for him.

The children watched this and soon began to get the idea that it was wrong to give Warm Fuzzies any time you were asked or felt like it. They too became very careful. They would watch their parents closely and whenever they felt that one of their parents was giving too many Fuzzies to others, they felt jealous and complained and sometimes even had a tantrum. And even though they found a Warm Fuzzy every time they reached into their bag they began to feel guilty whenever they gave them away so they reached in less and less and became more and more stingy with them.

Before the witch, people used to gather in groups of three, four or five, never caring too much who was giving Warm Fuzzies to whom. After the coming of the witch, people began to pair off and to reserve all their Warm Fuzzies for each other, exclusively. When people forgot to be careful and gave a Warm Fuzzy to just anybody they worried because they knew that somebody would probably resent sharing their Warm Fuzzies.

People began to give less and less Warm Fuzzies, and felt less warm and less fuzzy. They began to shrivel up and, occasionally, people would even die from lack of Warm Fuzzies. People felt worse and worse and, more and more, people went to the witch to buy potions and salves even though they didn't really seem to work.

Well, the situation was getting very serious indeed. The bad witch who had been watching all of this didn't really want the people to

*die (since dead people couldn't buy his salves and potions), so a
new plan was devised.*

*Everyone was given, free of charge, a bag that was very similar to
the Fuzzy Bag except that this one was cold while the Fuzzy Bag
was warm. Inside of the witch's bag were Cold Pricklies. These
Cold Pricklies did not make people feel warm and fuzzy; in fact
they made them feel cold and prickly instead. But the Cold Pricklies were better than nothing and they did prevent people's backs
from shriveling up.*

*So, from then on, when somebody asked for a Warm Fuzzy, people
who were worried about depleting their supply would say, 'I can't
give you a Warm Fuzzy, but would you like a Cold Prickly instead?'*

*Sometimes, two people would walk up to each other, thinking that
maybe they could get a Warm Fuzzy this time, but one of them
would change his mind and they would wind up giving each other
Cold Pricklies instead. So, the end result was that people were
not dying anymore but a lot of people were very unhappy and feeling very cold and prickly indeed.*

*The situation got very complicated since the coming of the witch
because there were fewer and fewer Warm Fuzzies around and
Warm Fuzzies which used to be as free as air, became extremely
valuable.*

*This caused people to do all sorts of things in order to get Warm
Fuzzies. People who could not find a generous partner had to
buy their Warm Fuzzies and had to work long hours to earn the
money.*

*Some people became 'popular' and got a lot of Warm Fuzzies
without having to give any back. These people would then sell
their Warm Fuzzies to people who were 'unpopular' and needed
them to feel that life was worth living.*

Another thing which happened was that some people would take Cold Pricklies – which were everywhere and freely available – and coated them white and fluffy so that they almost looked like Warm Fuzzies. These fake Warm Fuzzies were really Plastic Fuzzies, and they caused additional problems.

For instance, two or more people would get together and freely give each other Plastic Fuzzies. They expected to feel good, but they came away feeling bad instead. People got very confused never realizing that their cold, prickly feelings were because they had been given a lot of Plastic Fuzzies.

So the situation was very, very dismal and it all started because of the coming of the witch who made people believe that some day, when least expected, they might reach into their Warm Fuzzy Bag and find no more.

Not long ago, a young woman with big hips came to this unhappy land. She seemed not to have heard about the bad witch and was not worried about running out of Warm Fuzzies. She gave them out freely, even when not asked. They called her the Hip Woman and disapproved of her because she was giving the children the idea that they should not worry about running out of Warm Fuzzies. The children liked her very much because they felt good around her and they began to follow her example giving out Warm Fuzzies whenever they felt like it.

This made the grown-ups very worried. To protect the children from depleting their supplies of Warm Fuzzies they passed a law. The law made it a criminal offense to give out Warm Fuzzies in a reckless manner or without a license. Many children, however, seemed not to care; and in spite of the law they continued to give each other Warm Fuzzies whenever they felt like it and always when asked. Because there were many, many children, almost as *many as grown-ups, it began to look as if maybe they would have their way.*

As of now it's hard to say what will happen. Will the grown-ups' laws stop the recklessness of the children?

Are the grown-ups going to join with the Hip Woman and the children in taking a chance that there will always be as many Warm Fuzzies as needed?

Will they remember the days their children are trying to bring back when Warm Fuzzies were abundant because people gave them away freely?

The struggle spread all over the land and is probably going on right where you live. If you want to, and I hope you do, you can join by freely giving and asking for Warm Fuzzies and being as loving and healthy as you can.

So, what is this telling us about the world of business? We believe it is that one of the hurdles to staying sane in business is what Steiner calls the stroke economy; a system of social control that monitors the positive expressions of affection between people (see claudesteiner.com). Organisations are often set up in ways that create challenges to people having open, honest and appreciative relationships with each other. In fact, we think that organisations are especially prone to enforce the rules of the stroke economy and to create a scarcity of positive feelings by imposing the set of unwritten rules that govern the exchange of appreciation. This is how these unwritten rules play out:

1. **Don't give the appreciation of others that you would like to give** – If you do you will be suspected of being soft, brown-nosed, fluffy and weak, and you will run the risk of promoting a bloated sense of people's own self-importance.
2. **Don't ask for appreciation you would like to get** – You'll be told if you don't hear anything you should assume that all is OK. If

you go around asking for praise, people will think you are weak, needy and vulnerable.

3. **Don't accept appreciation that you would like to accept** – If someone compliments you, it's far better form to brush it off with a bit of dismissive humour than to take it on board. Accept appreciation and you will be seen as arrogant and conceited.

4. **Don't reject appreciation that you don't want if it's something that isn't in your interests** – That could be, for example, excessive compliments about your looks or a promotion to a position that takes you in the wrong direction for your career. To reject appreciation will mark you as being rude and ungrateful.

5. **Don't appreciate yourself** – Make sure that how good you feel about yourself totally depends on the feedback that you get and hold on to the view that you are only really as good as your last accomplishment. Otherwise you will be thought as conceited or arrogant.

In contrast, this is how we reinterpret Steiner's recommendations for use in organisations.

- Give the appreciation you want to give.
- Ask for and accept the appreciation you need.
- Reject the appreciation you don't want.
- Appreciate yourself.

The result if these precepts are applied in an organisation will be a heightened sense of mutual appreciation and increased morale and productivity.

These are simple ideas that might just work!

Top Tips for Relationships

- Think about how the SCARF model applies to you.
- Learn about Transactional Analysis.
- Try the PAC model.
- Reflect on your attachment patterns.
- Think about a relationship that feels stuck or difficult.
- Try Action Feeling Statements or Satir's Daily Temperature Reading on a relationship that really matters to you.
- If you have a coach, ask them more about perceptual positions or 'two-chair work' and have a go.
- Consider how a 'Warm Fuzzy Tale' might apply to your organisation.

Don't forget – there's more information for each tip in **Part 2** of this book (see pages 227–240) and online at **www.sane.works**

'If you want to conquer
the anxiety of life,
live in the moment,
live in the breath.'

– Amit Ray –

Part 1

Moods come and go like the weather. (Photo by DF)

We are emotional beings. If you didn't have feelings, you would find it exceptionally difficult to solve problems. The agility of the human brain depends as much on what is felt as what is thought.

It's true that there has been a lot written about emotional intelligence in recent years. It feels helpful that we can now have an open debate about leadership style and the effects on human performance. It's also good that we are more aware of the impact of potentially over-exercised strengths when we consider people for top jobs. All in all, we seem to be to be happier to accept that being at work involves feelings as much as thoughts.

Despite this, not a great deal has been written about mood at work. In everyday life we have an idea of what it's like to be in a good or bad mood but occupational psychologists – unlike their clinical, counselling and forensic counterparts – seem to have been quite nervous of this whole area. It's almost as if mood is considered as little more than unhelpful noise in the system.

When we looked at personality in Chapter 1, we saw that one useful concept was that of emotional stability and we talked about the idea of derailment.

But mood is a different matter: it's the everyday variation of how we feel and is not necessarily connected with the extreme edges of our personalities. Being sensitive to our own emotions, registering the emotions of others, communicating with positive impact, being resistant to stress and staying positive and constructive, these are all seen as good things – but with mood, the message is less clear.

Equally, in business, coaches seem just as wary. The emphasis seems to have been on the maintenance of positivity in the face of challenge and in the development of robustness and resilience. It's almost as if mood has no real place and that it's just a label for irrationality.

Leadership development experts like to borrow ideas from the battlefield or sports field so they too have enthusiastically embraced the idea of mental toughness. As a coping strategy we think this is excellent, but there's a risk of over-application. Taken too far, we run the risk of seeing moods as simply unhelpful interference from the dark sides of who we are and as aspects of ourselves that should be controlled and managed more than listened to and nurtured. In short, the message could easily be heard as 'be less moody'!

In this chapter, we are looking at the moods that we have in relation to the normal ups and downs of business life and not at the level of personal distress that might cause you to seek out the help of a counsellor or therapist. Nevertheless, we want to explore moods in more depth and apply some more of the perspectives of psychotherapy.

Let's start with the raw material of moods – emotions. Imagine boiling everything down to just four emotions, as described by psychotherapist Adrienne Lee.

- Fear
- Sadness
- Anger
- Joy

We are particularly interested in the first three because these emotions create moods, which can, in turn, negatively affect the way you function at work. On the whole, we'd maintain that joy is a good thing! Rather than banishing moods to the corporate naughty corner, we are interested in exploring them further and in understanding how you can harness them to your advantage.

Here's what we have included in this chapter.

- **How you take in information** – Our exploration starts with discussing what you are aware of and how you initially process information as this has a profound impact on your emotions and mood.
- **How you make emotion-based decisions** – The next stage is to look at the different brain systems we use in decision-making. We don't think one model is better than another and we all have our favourites, but looking at this area in different ways can be very enlightening.

- **Vulnerability and authenticity** – Here we talk about the extent to which you own your feelings and how sometimes you may distance yourself from them – or even cover one set of feelings up with another. We think that some of these internal feelings battles can have a huge impact on your mood.
- **The link between thoughts and feelings** – This is discussed in depth in one school of therapy and coaching, so we pay this a visit.
- **Resilience** – An important element that we don't want to ignore, so this is covered too.
- **Mindfulness and anchoring** – We want, of course, to make this chapter as practical as possible so we explore two techniques that you can use to be aware of your moods and feelings but not act on them unthinkingly.

Filtering Incoming Information

We like to think we are rational beings, objectively taking in information through our five senses, processing it and then acting accordingly. Unfortunately, we don't quite work like that. Even the information that we receive is heavily filtered.

Our filters work by deleting, distorting or generalising what comes in. There are whole schools of cognitive psychology devoted to this topic and it's well beyond the scope of this book to go into great detail but here's the minimum it's helpful to know.

Deletion

Deletion is where you pay selective attention. It would be impossible to be fully aware of every bit of information that impinges on your consciousness and so you build up mini programmes or 'schemas' that allow you to process the world in chunks.

As we explored in the previous chapter, the brain is a huge consumer of energy and it's also constantly primed to detect threat. It makes sense for you to be able to access information rapidly and efficiently and, for the most part, a quick and dirty appreciation of your world serves you well. This is why you can drive different cars and operate computer programs without the need for a manual. Things have a predictability about them, which allows you to operate without continual conscious thought.

But, as with all programming, things can go amiss. Deleting information can have a significant impact on your mood. Paying only selective attention can cause biases that are undesirable, ranging from depression through to prejudice. At such times, you fail to pay attention to positive data, falling into the trap instead of encoding everything according to a limited number of negative categories. This is sometimes called confirmation bias. You might hold the view, therefore, that the world is a bleak and hostile place and few good things happen to you. When they do, you don't notice them. Or you believe that certain racial groups always have the same attributes, ignoring data to the contrary when you come across an individual who doesn't seem to fit into the mould.

It follows, therefore, that one way of dealing with deleted information is to become more aware of what is happening in the moment – to literally expand your conscious awareness. There's more about this in the Mindfulness section (see page 146).

Distortion

As the name suggests, this is where you misrepresent reality. It could be that you perceive things that are simply not there – or at least that nobody else is able to see, hear, feel, touch or smell. You might even complain that your mind is playing tricks on you but, of course, all of this can happen completely out of your conscious awareness.

Psychologists talk about distortions as biases of thought (or 'cognition' if they are trying to impress you) and one of the goals of therapy can be to help clients identify and own patterns of thoughts, feelings or behaviour that seem particularly dominant.

If you Google 'cognitive biases' you will come across a Wikipedia entry that includes a long list. You will recognise some of them immediately and we explore the patterns that seem to have a direct impact on your mood in more detail below.

We have already talked about your brain being an uncertainty-reduction machine. In fact, to experience a situation in which you end up entertaining two or more contradictory beliefs is psychologically painful. The evidence is that you will act to bring things back into line and if that involves distorting reality, so be it. Psychologists call this cognitive dissonance.

As with many things in psychology, the phenomenon of cognitive dissonance has been known about for a long time, and well before someone decided to give it a posh name. Sour grapes? The phrase actually comes from Aesop's Fables in which a fox sees some tasty-looking grapes that are high up in a tree. The reality of the grapes and the reality of not being able to get at them are both present in the fox's mind and the only way to resolve the conflict is to devalue the grapes by concluding that they are probably sour!

In therapy and coaching, we talk about one type of distortion, which is called discounting. A discount is when you minimise some aspect of yourself, of others or of the reality of a situation. What you do with a discount is maintain a sense of identity or personal narrative and resist changes to your frame of reference.

Let's say, for example, that you see yourself as working class. You might hold certain beliefs about what this means, some of which could be limiting. Let's say that you are attracted to the idea of becoming a barrister. You could hold the view that this is an attractive career, interesting and potentially well paid, but the chance of getting a pupillage after a bar vocational course is slim unless you are from a privileged background. So you now have a choice, stick with your ambitions and trust that someone will recognise the talents that you have or decide on a different career. If you do the former, you will have to challenge your frame of reference. If you do the latter, you will have to challenge the attractiveness of being a barrister in the first place.

What discounts do is both protect you and limit your choice. The protection to your sense of self comes from the maintenance of a safe position. After all, all personal growth involves risk. What you are embarking on might not work and the people who surround you may not be supportive of the new you.

Discounts work at four levels. Building up awareness of which ones you tend to employ can be very useful.

- **Existence** – If you discount at this level you either don't notice what's happening around you, you fail to see something as a problem or you are not aware of the options. Let's say you are driving down the motorway and a red light appears on your dashboard. You might not actually see this but you could also turn a blind eye to it. If you do see it, you might not recognise it as a problem and, instead, carry on driving. If you see it and register that it's important, you might carry on driving anyway because you don't feel that you have a choice, not realising that you could pull over and call a car breakdown service for some help.

- **Significance** – If you discount at this level you are aware of the existence of a stimulus but you minimise its level of threat to you. In other words, you trivialise something that should be taken seriously. This is an area of particular interest to professionals engaged in healthcare. Let's say you are an overweight, middle-aged smoker. You are fully aware of all of these facts. There's no denying that you have put on some weight over the years, that you are 49 and that there are several empty packets of cigarettes in your wastepaper bin. You are also aware that climbing up stairs leaves you out of breath but you console yourself with the knowledge that you are in better shape than many of your friends down the pub and that your Uncle Fred lived to be 85 and had a lifestyle that was far less healthy than yours. After all, don't most guys in their later 40s get a bit breathless at times just from everyday living? If you did this you'd be discounting the importance of your symptoms.

- **Change possibility** – If you discount at this level you are aware of what's happening and you recognise the significance and seriousness of it but you don't feel change is possible. Let's use another example. We'll assume for this one that you are feeling depressed. You have felt down for a while and, in particular, you are getting little enjoyment from your job. The problem is that you don't believe that change is really a possibility. Instead, you think that this is the best you can and should hope for and you are lucky to have employment during a period of economic instability.

- **Personal ability** – If you discount at this level you are getting personal. You hold the belief that either you or someone else cannot react differently to a given situation; that you or they cannot solve problems or that you or they cannot exercise choice. Let's imagine a particularly difficult person at your place of work. You would like them to behave differently but if you discount at this level, you will say that they can't help being who they are, that they are 'wired up that way' or that it's your job to work around them.

- **Generalisation** – This is where we draw global conclusions on the basis of a limited amount of data. In other words, we discount the exceptions to the norm. This is actually the way we all learn and it's fascinating listening to small children do this. But it's not always helpful as adults and it can lead to limiting beliefs, a restricted way of seeing the world and a real rigidity in the way that we think. Prejudice is a good example here.

Generalisation can also prop up moods that don't help us; tipping over into what therapists call grandiosity. Take bipolar disorder, for example. The manic phase of this mental state is often associated with larger-than-life fantasies regarding power, position, influence and entitlement. And we are all familiar with people who talk of 'everyone', 'all the time', 'never' when they are referring to things that bother them. Strictly speaking, we shouldn't have just written 'we are all familiar' for rather obvious reasons, but you get the drift!

Other Filters

And it doesn't end there! You also have beliefs, expectations, culture and patterns of thought that have been laid down as you grew up. We looked at some of these in Chapter 2. Let's not forget the role of language either. The words we use describe the experiences we have but, of course, the words are not the actual experiences, just representations of them. It stands to reason that if we don't have a word for something, our experience of whatever it is will be different than if we do. Again, this can have a direct impact on our feelings and mood.

Processing and Different Brain Systems

Having discussed how we take in information, the question then arises as to how we process it. You could think of your brain as being composed of a number of discrete systems – some operating at an unconscious level as reflexes, some connected with emotions, and some with thinking or higher mental processing.

Reflexes

At the level of basic physiology, there are some features of the way we process information about the world that we have no control over at all. You don't need to consciously think or feel anything for these systems to kick in.

For example, when shown a sexually arousing picture we cannot help it that our pupils dilate. Equally, when shown a picture that is threatening and disturbing, we cannot help it that our pupils contract. Skilled readers of body language know this and the myriad of other cues that indicate how we process information at a physical level. Your body doesn't know how to lie!

Of course, there's not much that you can do to override reflexes, but what you can do is pay attention to what your body is telling you. The clues that you get may help you manage your mood.

To live in the world is to experience feelings and the only place that you can have feelings is in your body. If you find it hard to put your feelings into words, a good habit is to check where in your body any sensations are being experienced. In the face of something that's stressful or upsetting, you might feel tense across your shoulders, your head may feel light and your stomach could be churning. Oddly, these sensations can occur even if you claim not to be experiencing any emotions at all. This could be because you are suppressing your emotions consciously or unconsciously.

Doctors and psychologists sometimes call a painful or uncomfortable sensation that a patient complains of but which has no apparent physical cause, a somatisation. Common sites appear to be the digestive, nervous and reproductive systems, with patients often reporting very high levels of anxiety in relation to their symptoms. If you experience sensations in your body that have no apparent cause, it could be wise to examine the circumstances in which they arise and to wonder if they could provide you with some useful information.

Emotions and Thoughts

The next system to consider is that which processes emotion. Again, this system doesn't need conscious thought to activate it but thought can certainly make it spring into life.

Many of you will be familiar with Daniel Goleman's publications on emotional intelligence and the brilliant job that he has made of stating a case for EQ (emotional quotient) being more important than IQ (intelligence quotient). But the actual idea of brain structures devoted to emotional processing, the so-called limbic system, goes back over 60 years. By the way, as is often the case, it wasn't actually Goleman who came up with the idea of emotional intelligence as a psychological theory. It was two other guys called Salovey and Mayer, whom everyone seems to have forgotten about.

Regardless of the fine points of neuroanatomy and who coined what phrase, the metaphor of the emotional brain has proven to be really useful. It's now accepted that Goleman's five components of emotional intelligence – self-awareness, self-regulation, internal motivation, empathy and social skills – are, at the very least, useful ways of talking about how we process emotions in a workplace context.

Recently, another commentator has appeared on the scene and he has skilfully described the tension that so often exists within our competing brain systems. Dr Steve Peters, a British psychiatrist, has created an entertaining and highly readable model of mental life in his book *The Chimp Paradox*.

What Dr Peters does with consummate skill, and a touch of humour not usually associated with psychiatrists, is talk about emotional processing using the metaphor of a chimpanzee. The 'Chimp' is actually a representation of the human limbic system. That's the brain structures that glory in the names of telencephalon, diencephalon and mesencephalon. This includes the olfactory bulbs, hippocampus, amygdala, anterior thalamic nuclei, fornix, columns of fornix, mammillary body, septum pellucidum, habenular commissure, cingulate gyrus, parahippocampal gyrus, limbic cortex, and limbic midbrain areas. Not surprising that he chose the label 'Chimp' then – it's a little easier to remember!

The 'Chimp' lives alongside another brain system which Dr Peters calls the Human. This is roughly equivalent to the higher brain functions, which are located in the neocortex. You are the Human in this metaphor and locked in your head is your 'Chimp'.

There's a big difference between how the Human and the 'Chimp' think.

The Human:

- Works with plans and weighs up different courses of action.
- Favours logical thinking.
- Works with here-and-now problem solving.
- Is interested in facts and truth, evidence and rational arguments.
- Acts in context and in a measured and proportionate way.
- Is comfortable with shades of grey.
- Processes information relatively slowly.

The 'Chimp', on the other hand, is a different character altogether. Your 'Chimp':

- Works with feelings and impressions.
- Favours emotional thinking.
- Tends to jump to conclusions.
- Is acutely interested in moving away from threat and towards reward.
- Pays less attention to context and can be impulsive.
- Thinks in black and white.
- Is influenced by past feelings as much as what's happening right now.
- Processes information in a quick and dirty way.

You might conclude at first glance that any 'Chimp'-type behaviour is best avoided as it's going to get you into serious trouble. The problem is that your 'Chimp' is part of you or, to put it another way, you are essentially an emotional being. All of the information that comes from your senses arrives at your 'Chimp' first and you can't overpower your emotional system as, like a chimpanzee, it's five times stronger than you are! All you can do is manage your responses and this means recognising your feelings in the first place. There's a lot more in Dr Peters' book and he goes on to describe how we store information, retrieve it and how we can re-programme ourselves.

So where is this taking us? If you are to stay sane at work you have to come to terms with eight facts.

1. You have emotions, feelings, moods. You aren't just a collection of thoughts!
2. It's your responsibility to manage your feelings and moods, not just act upon them.
3. And the first step in managing anything is to recognise, accept and own its existence.

4. Denying your feelings will get you into worse trouble than acting on them without thought – in the long run at least!

5. You can build up your awareness of the typical biases of judgement that arise from purely emotional thinking.

6. The system works backwards as well as forwards, so what you feel can be subject to what you think but what you think can just as easily influence how you feel.

7. It's not a good idea to be passive; a bit of active management in this area goes a long way.

8. You can learn techniques that help your emotional and rational brains (or your 'Chimp' and Human) work in relative harmony.

Owning Your Feelings

You might be very receptive to your feelings. On the other hand, you might have become rather adept at ignoring them or pushing them out of conscious awareness. In Chapter 2, we talked about psychological drivers, in particular the desire to be strong. But it's not just people having this as a prominent driver who are affected. We all defend ourselves against unacceptable feelings, particularly feelings of vulnerability, by employing cunning psychological defences. You might recognise any or all of the following common ones.

- **Repression** – This is where you unconsciously block the feelings and thoughts that are unacceptable to you. When you have repressed material, it's very hard to gain access to it and much of early psychotherapy was interested in helping people come to terms with what they had repressed so that it could be digested and neutralised and so that it could no longer cause distress and damage.

- **Denial** – You will have heard people say, 'He's in denial'. Denial is the refusal to accept something that is happening and that is visible to others. Psychotherapists often call this a primitive defence mechanism because it is characteristic of how small children behave. It's not uncommon to see this mechanism being used by people with addiction problems such as alcohol, drugs ... or work.

- **Regression** – This is all about going back to an earlier stage of development than the one that you are in now. 'Oh, do grow up,' you might hear people say to others who seem to be using regression to cope with something that is stressful.

- **Displacement** – Again, this one has passed into everyday speech as we talk about *displacement activities*, which is the pattern of behaviour that you recognise in yourself and others when you or they don't want to do something. This is all about redirecting your thoughts and feelings about one person, object or situation onto another. Take anger, for example. This is a classic emotion that is displaced rather than owned and the danger is that you take it out on innocent people or even your family pet as they become the target for feelings that you really have about someone or something else!

- **Dissociation** – This is when you lose connection with yourself. You could have thoughts and feelings that seem separate from you. You might recall memories without their emotional components, almost as if you were an observer looking in. This defence mechanism is commonly seen in extreme trauma where recalling a deeply troubling event is more than you can cope with.

- **Projection** – This is where you take some aspect of yourself that is unacceptable to you and attribute it to someone else. What this often looks like is blaming or criticising. When you do this you don't realise that you are the projector and it's your material that you can see.

- **Acting out** – In order to express thoughts or feelings the person feels incapable of otherwise expressing, they act out a scenario. You could hit an inanimate object as a way of expressing how you feel. If you have experience of small children, you will recognise this one from the 'terrible twos'!

- **Intellectualisation** – This is where you coldly think about something rather than feel it. You might use sanitised language or you might refer to your feelings in a cut off and abstract way. If someone asks you how you are feeling, if you are using this defence mechanism, you will come back with a thought.

Wrong Labels

There are many other ways in which you can defend yourself against your feelings but before we leave this, it's interesting to look at one last twist in the tale. It might be that you are very aware of your feelings but that you are not really recognising them for what they are. When you were growing up you would have wanted attention, love and recognition but some feelings would not have been as welcome by your caregivers as others. If this was the case, in order to get your needs met, you would have learnt to select another feeling instead. In our work as coaches, we see this a lot in male executives where sadness and vulnerability are not feelings that they are comfortable having. What they tend to reach for instead is anger, thereby confirming that indeed big boys don't cry but it's OK to throw your weight around!

CBT

If you receive psychological support via the UK National Health Service, the chances are that you will have cognitive behavioural therapy (CBT) as part of your treatment package. Some years ago, this approach even found its way into corporate life via the coaching community, so we now have Cognitive Behavioural Coaching or CBC as well (see the Resources Chapter for a good book reference from the 'Dummies' series – we kid you not!).

The central argument in CBT or CBC is that how we think dictates how we feel and that under stress and pressure, our thinking patterns can become seriously distorted. We feel there's a lot of truth in this, so it seems worth sharing these patterns with you. Here are the top patterns that we see in our work. All of these represent examples of rigidity of thought.

Rigidity of Thought

Thought pattern	Characteristics
Catastrophising	You might remember Frazer from the British 1970s sitcom Dad's Army? Skilfully played with wild, rolling eyes by the actor John Laurie, James Frazer was quick to make a drama out of a crisis! If you are catastrophising, this is how you are behaving: you are imagining the worst possible outcome and there's no sense of proportion in how you are processing things.
All-or-nothing thinking	This is a black-and-white way of thinking; there are no shades of grey. If you listen to someone who is thinking this way, there will be all sorts of false dilemmas and grandiose statements in what they say. You are likely to hear 'never', 'always'. Psychologists sometimes call this thinking pattern 'splitting'. The object of thought is all good or all bad.
Fortune telling	When you are doing this, you know exactly how the future is going to pan out and it's usually not well! There's no reality testing, no consideration of an alternative outcome; you just know how things are going to be!
Mind reading	The personalised version of fortune telling, this is where you believe that you can get inside someone's head. Mistake – nobody can. You might be inferring deep and dark motives from someone's body language and you act without any verification of your suspicions. This is the seat of paranoia.

Thought pattern	Characteristics
Emotional reasoning	This is where your 'Chimp' has taken over completely. We all act from the heart rather than the head from time to time, but with emotional reasoning, you mistake feelings for thoughts. Faced with something that makes you anxious, for example, your anxiety is mislabelled as a harbinger of impending doom, rather than just a feeling.
Overgeneralising	If it's true once, it's always true if you think this way. Let's say you try your hand at sales and you get rejected. Instead of looking at the specifics of a situation, you decide that all prospective customers will behave this way. This takes us on to ...
Labelling	You are not a label! It's interesting that if you ask a person what they do (verb) for a living they will always come back with a label (noun). This might make for simpler conversations, but taken to extremes, it can be very limiting. Notice when the label is also discounted – 'I'm just a secretary' for example. The same goes for statements of self-worth like 'I'm useless'.
Disqualifying the positives	The English are good at this. 'Nice dress' you say, 'Oh this old thing? I've had it ages,' is the response. 'Great result,' you shout. 'It was a fluke,' comes the reply! Learning to gracefully take positive feedback is something we spend a lot of time on with our clients!
Personalising	This is an extreme attribution where people are seen free of context. Thus, things become 'all my fault' or 'all your fault' and the environment is ignored.

Low frustration tolerance	Between 1990 and 2000, the Scottish actor, Richard Wilson played the archetypal grumpy old man in his portrayal of Victor Meldrew in the BBC sitcom *One Foot in the Grave*. A complex and tragicomic figure, Meldrew came to represent all that it is to suffer from the continual frustrations of everyday life. Going back further, you might remember Basil Fawlty, so brilliantly acted by John Cleese in *Fawlty Towers*. The common denominator of both characters is the complete inability to shrug off the setbacks and minor irritants that beset us all.

Managing Moods

Managing your mood is about recognising the feelings you have, owning them and then soothing yourself when you become agitated. Soothing sounds like a term that belongs to childcare and that's no accident. If responsive and nurturing parents brought you up, you would have experienced attunement. This is where your caregiver acted as your emotional thermostat and showed you how to control your feelings. As we discussed in Chapter 3, if your caregiver was absent, inattentive or unpredictably available, you would not have been so lucky.

If you are feeling a bit sceptical about the last statement and need further evidence regarding the role of parenting and attunement in mood management, have a look at the 'Still Face Experiment' on YouTube.

Any work on self-development needs to begin with emotional control. If you can't do this and you are at the mercy of a swirling mass of thoughts, feelings and fears, progress is that much more difficult. It is for this reason that we start a lot of therapeutic work with grounding techniques.

Firstly, we will look at mindfulness, then meditation (although the two really go hand in hand) and then a little technique called anchoring.

Mindfulness

This ancient practice seems to be everywhere these days. Proponents claim that it's more than a set of skills and that it's a philosophy of life – an approach which involves paying attention to the present moment in a non-judgemental and accepting way. Mindfulness is something that can be used during many day-to-day activities, from walking to work to eating your lunch.

Put simply, mindfulness is tuning into what is all around you and cultivating the skill of looking at anything with a degree of detachment – and that includes yourself.

Mindfulness is helpful in managing stress, anxiety, worry and low mood, as it provides a way of paying attention in a focused but non-judgemental way to the here-and-now. This is opposed to allowing ourselves to become tied up in the unhelpful thoughts that can often follow challenging life events (for example, underperforming on a project at work, failing to get a promotion). Often, when we experience such a challenging life event, it is our thoughts about that event that lead to the difficult emotions we all experience from time to time, including fear, sadness and anger. Mindfulness acknowledges these thoughts but teaches a non-judgemental and accepting approach to them that allows you to 'let them go' when your mind invariably moves on to other things.

The kind of awareness of our thoughts and emotions that mindfulness teaches is very helpful, as sometimes the way we think about events, and even process information, is not unbiased but skewed in some way. This can particularly be the case if we hold some unhelpful beliefs about ourselves, the world or other people.

Melanie Fennell – a Clinical Psychologist and internationally renowned expert in the area of low self-esteem – offers a helpful way of thinking generally about how we may process and interpret information in a way that is shaped by our beliefs and if ... then rules. In short, Melanie proposes that our beliefs about ourselves (such as, I'm a worthwhile person, or I'm useless), the world (other people are caring, other people can't be trusted) and our future (I'm capable of getting a pro-motion, I will fail at anything I try), and the if ... then rules which exist to protect us from negative beliefs in these areas (for example, a person with the belief that they are stupid might develop the if ... then rule of 'If I succeed at everything I do, then I'm competent') can skew how we process and interpret information.

For example, consider person A, who thinks 'I'm a stupid person', and has the if ... then rule of 'If I work hard and succeed at everything then I'm not a stupid person'. If they don't perform well on a small part of a project but perform well during the vast majority of the project, they will be more likely to attend to the information about things they haven't done well. Also, they will likely interpret this information in a biased way so that, rather than having a balanced appraisal of their performance ('it is not feasible to excel at everything all the time, my performance was partly dependent on other people who did not per-form well either'), they will view their performance as indicating that they are incompetent, stupid or somehow inadequate. This is because such information, and the interpretation of that information, is con-sistent with person A's beliefs about themselves. This kind of biased attention, processing and interpretation of information is called a 'cognitive filter', and can manifest in several ways.

- We tend to attend to and process information, which is consistent with our beliefs about ourselves, the world and our futures.

- We often ignore information, which is inconsistent with our be-liefs about ourselves, the world and our futures.

- Ambiguous information, which is seemingly neither in support of, nor contradicts our beliefs, is contorted to support our beliefs about the world, our futures and ourselves.

- We are more likely to remember information which fits with our beliefs, as we were more likely to attend to and process it in the first place.

ABC of Mindfulness

Mindfulness is a beautifully simple antidote to all of this. The writer and mindfulness teacher Ed Halliwell talks of mindfulness as being an ABC approach to life:

- **A is awareness** – This is about being fully aware of what's happening in the current moment: your thoughts, feelings and bodily sensations.

- **B is being with** – Experiencing the thought, the feeling or the sensation and not deflecting it, denying it or suppressing it, this is also about staying with something without attachment. What often happens in life is that we become aware of something that disturbs us, either finding the feeling unacceptable or worrying that it will be overwhelming. Because of this, we fail to mentally digest what's bothering us. But the undigested material mentally regurgitates as it demands our attention. If we stay with something and don't push it away, the opposite happens: we find a way of dealing with it.

- **C is choice** – Accepting that you have a choice about how you deal with the circumstances you encounter and whether you live your life on autopilot. In his book, *A New Earth*, Eckhart Tolle makes a wonderfully liberating observation. Tolle argues that we are not our thoughts and our feelings. If we were just our feelings we'd be like the 'Chimp' in Steve Peters' book. If we were just our thoughts, we'd not be able to stand outside ourselves and recognise that we have thoughts. Regardless of the brand of coaching or therapy, most disciplines encourage us to develop an observing ego: something that can appraise our thoughts, needs, wants, desires and compulsions.

So when you are being mindful, you become an observer of who you are. You notice that you have thoughts and feelings that come and go but you aren't those thoughts and feelings. For example, instead of saying 'I am angry' you could say 'I feel anger'. You are the observer of the emotion and although you own the feeling you are not all-consumed by it and you are still free to choose how you act. In the words of Sri Nisargadatta Maharaj, an Indian sage and author of *I Am That*:

> *Discover all that you are not – body, feelings, thoughts, time, space, this or that – nothing, concrete or abstract, which you perceive can be you. The very act of perceiving shows that you are not what you perceive.*

If this all sounds a bit abstract, try thinking about the precepts upon which mindfulness is built and learn to meditate.

- **Open-minded curiosity** – simply stopping, breathing and reflecting on what you are thinking and feeling. What are those patterns of thoughts that are going through your head? Do they have a familiar ring to them? What are you feeling right now? Where in your body do you have this feeling?
- **Acceptance** – Not censoring what you are thinking and feeling. Don't push a thought or feeling aside but simply accept it. There's no need to try and change it. Just be fully aware.
- **Compassion and non-judgement** – Being kind to yourself. If the hectoring voice of your internal critical parent makes itself known, listen to it and hear it out. Don't resist it or act in self-defence. You are in no danger and you don't need to think or feel anything in order to be acceptable. Simply experience all that you are.
- **Patience** – Taking your time. There's no rush and there is nothing wrong with stepping away and allowing yourself to be.
- **Trust** – Yourself!
- **Letting go** – If you feel like holding onto something that is a pleasant experience, be prepared to let it go and accept that something else good will come along to take its place. Cultivate a philosophy of abundance and not scarcity.

And if at this point you'd like an illustration, how about this metaphorical story by Portia Nelson? It's called 'An Autobiography in Five Short Chapters' from *There's a Hole in My Sidewalk: The Romance of Self-Discovery* by Portia Nelson.

Chapter 1

I walk down the street.

There is a deep hole in the sidewalk.

I fall in.

I am lost ... I am helpless.

It isn't my fault.

It takes forever to find a way out.

Chapter 2

I walk down the same street.

There is a deep hole in the sidewalk.

I pretend I don't see it.

I fall in again.

I can't believe I am in the same place.

But, it isn't my fault.

It still takes me a long time to get out.

Chapter 3

I walk down the same street.

There is a deep hole in the sidewalk.

I see it is there.

I still fall in ... it's a habit ... but,
My eyes are open.

I know where I am.

It is my fault.

I get out immediately.

Chapter 4

I walk down the same street.

There is a deep hole in the sidewalk.

I walk around it.

Chapter 5

I walk down another street.

Learning to Meditate

One way to refine your mindfulness skills is to meditate. There's no need to book into a retreat and eat lentils for a week in a Buddhist monastery – unless you want to, of course! There are simple practices that, in combination with the ideas above, you can incorporate into your daily life. You might find these easier to learn in a class but there are lots of audio guides around and a number of online courses.

The simplest way of learning to meditate is to be mindful of your breathing. You can do this for a few minutes or for an hour. If you want to keep an eye on time, download an app to your smartphone. Just search for 'meditation timer' and you will find a whole host to choose from.

Find somewhere quiet and comfortable where you won't be disturbed and if you are using a smartphone timer, don't forget to put your phone onto flight mode. It's not necessary to kneel on the floor but a comfortable chair where you can sit upright is necessary. Try to avoid being scrunched up or in any position where your breathing is restricted. It's also better to be sitting up than lying down – you may well fall asleep if you try this in a horizontal position!

All you now need to do is focus on your breathing. A way to do this is to count the number of incoming breaths in cycles of ten. Do this ten times. Then focus on your outgoing breaths in the same cycles of ten. There's something about counting that initially helps. Next, simply focus on your breath. Feel it in your nose, your throat, your chest and down to your diaphragm. Try to feel your breath as low down in your body as you can. The more you focus your breath on your stomach area, the more grounding and calming the effect it has. When you are anxious, you do the opposite, with all your breathing being shallow and high up.

Now comes the mindfulness bit. Your mind is going to wander as you do this. You might well lose count of your breaths or you might become aware of thoughts and feelings; hopes, dreams, fears and desires... it's fine if this happens. Simply accept the sensations and then very gently guide your wandering mind back on track. There's no failure and no rush; it's all a matter of practice. Slowly but surely what you will find is that your periods of focus on your breathing get longer and the number of intrusive thoughts slowly diminishes. Do this for a week at about the same time each day and notice the difference.

The nice thing about mindfulness is that you really don't need to sit crossed-legged to do it at all. As a practice, it can be incorporated into anything you do. It's all about being fully present in whatever you are doing.

- **Walk mindfully** – Try noticing the physical sensations of walking: the pattern of pressure on the soles of your feet, the sensation of your breathing, what you can see, hear and smell around you. So much the better if your walk is in a beautiful, tranquil place but it could just as easily be around your office. Try heightening the sensation by doing this barefoot, if that's appropriate!

- **Eat mindfully** – Instead of bolting down your sandwich as you take your lunch 'al-desko' with the crumbs dropping onto your keyboard, try stopping for a moment and noticing what you are eating. Look at it, smell it and really taste it. Feel the sensation of swallowing your food and take twice as long over eating it. There's even a secondary benefit to this one as eating more slowly often means that you will eat less. If you have been on one of our seminars, you will have experienced mindful eating of a raisin!

- **Stop and listen mindfully** – It doesn't matter where you are – on the train, in the car or sitting in front of your laptop – there will be sounds that you aren't aware of. We habituate and filter out noise all the time but it's still there. Paying attention to your surroundings can feel very different. Try doing this for just one minute.

In case you think that mindfulness all sounds a bit too spiritual or New Age, you might be interested to know that one of the most prolific writers on the subject is Dr John Kabat-Zin. He's a scientist through and through and his application of Buddhist principles to stress-reduction is extremely well researched. It was Kabat-Zin who brought mindfulness into medicine, downplaying any religious connections but at the same time showing how the practice can be used to alleviate physical and mental pain.

Kabat-Zin has a simple and clear definition of mindfulness:

Mindfulness means paying attention in a particular way; on purpose, in the present moment, and non-judgmentally.

We have a friend who puts it even more succinctly. As an ex-advertising man, he has a wonderful knack of encapsulating the essence of things with the minimum of words. His view of mindfulness practice is just two characters: '.b'. The full stop invites us to do just that: stop. The 'b' is for breath. Just stop and breathe.

Anchoring

This is a little technique from NLP and sports psychology. It's all about invoking a positive mental state and using it as a resource in the present – a sort of conditioned reflex. The idea is that your feelings are influenced by your thoughts and your thoughts are impacted on by your feelings.

The great thing about NLP is that it's process driven. You learn a technique and you apply it so that you get better and better all the time. That's the essence of many a skill – practice.

Anchoring can work really well for anxiety. Let's say you are facing an important event and this is making you feel nervous when you want to feel relaxed and in control. Public speaking and presentations are typical events that our clients tell us make them uncomfortable. Every time you think about the upcoming event, your stomach knots, you feel sweaty and you start to breathe rapid, shallow breaths. You imagine tripping over your words, everyone looking critically at you and the whole thing going belly up. The more you tell yourself not to think these things, the worse it gets.

Stop! You can't fight your inner 'Chimp'! Remember, it's much stronger than you are. Worse still, your unconscious mind can't process a negative command. In order to stop thinking about the thing that's bothering you, you need to think about it first. By trying to push it away, you are unwittingly strengthening the negative association. You need to do some step-by-step re-programming by stealth.

- **Imagine a state of relaxation** – Think about a time when you were really relaxed. Pick your most vivid example: something that engages as many of your senses as possible. Recall the sights, sounds, smells, tastes and feelings of touch.

- **Turn up the volume on the memory** – Imagine it as though it is a video replay. Make the colours of the visual memory stronger. Make the image bigger and stronger. Bring the image closer to you so that it fills all of your visual field. Do the same with your other senses. Find a keyword tag that sums up the experience: a strong, positive affirmation that makes you feel good.

- **Attach the feelings to a physical sensation** – When the feelings associated with the memory are at their strongest, anchor those feelings to a physical action. Touching a knuckle is often a good one, or you could pull an earlobe or stroke the back of your neck. This is your anchor.

- **Strengthen your anchor** – Repeat this a few times until you have really strengthened your anchor.
- **Rehearse the event** – Now mentally rehearse the upcoming event whilst firing your anchor by using the physical sensation. Keep doing this until you get the result you are looking for.
- **Fire your anchor** – Feel free to fire your anchor in the event itself.
- **Stay observant** – The chances are, sooner or later you are going to notice other people doing this too.

Pulling It All Together – Resilience

Before we move on, it feels worthwhile to say something about resilience: another term that seems very much in vogue. The label 'resilience' seems to have replaced stress management and wellbeing. The problem is, it's still not very clear what we mean by it. A bit like the word 'authentic', as applied to leadership, resilience is a hard one to pin down. We think the best, simple definition goes back to 2004 when two psychologists called Tugade and Fredrickson stated:

Psychological resilience refers to effective coping and adaptation when faced with loss, hardship or adversity.

For us, what this means is a bit of biology, a fair amount of personality and quite a lot of learnt behaviours. We particularly like the model of resilience that has been created by UK psychologists at Robertson Cooper (RCL). You can try this out for yourself by completing their on-line questionnaire, which is called *i-resilience* (www.robertsoncooper. com/iresilience). The RCL model has, as we interpret it, four parts to it.

- **Confidence** – Connected with feeling competent, effective and having a good level of self-esteem, to be resilient, you need to feel good about yourself and to be self-confident. You could say this is all about being able to call up positive emotions and keep negative feelings in perspective. Cross-reference this part of the model with the first chapter of this book.

- **Social support** – It's no use being confident if you are on your own and cut off from other people. This is why the model places a great deal of emphasis on the network of relationships that you have around you. The more you can lean appropriately on others for support, the more resilient you are likely to be.
- **Adaptability** – Remember Philippa Perry's point at the start of this book? The RCL model also majors on being adaptable, as does pretty much all of coaching and psychotherapy.
- **Purposefulness** – This part of the model is all about living your life on purpose. You can stand the everyday knocks if you are doing something which has a clear sense of purpose. Ask any top athlete what spurs them on.

There's a lot to commend the RCL model, particularly as they set the whole thing in an organisational context and stress the importance of the environment in which you are working just as much as your own make-up. No matter how personally resilient you are, life is going to be that much easier if you work for an organisation where:

- You have the necessary training, equipment and information to do your job.
- The culture is one of collaboration rather than competition and individualism.
- Change is managed well.
- Some thought is given to your workload and your boss doesn't just keep piling it on with no consideration of what's humanly possible.
- You have some say in how things are done.
- There's a clear reason for what you are doing and a sense of meaning and purpose.

The other thing we like about RCL is that they make a lot of their material available free of charge. This seems very much in keeping with an organisation that sets out to promote more psychologically healthy workplaces.

Happiness

We didn't want to leave this chapter on mood without mentioning the whole area of happiness. *The World Happiness Report (WHR) 2013*, edited by Helliwell, Layard and Sachs, makes interesting reading, particularly Chapter 3, which addresses mental illness and unhappiness. The great thing about the WHR is it is a relatively hard-nosed analysis of the causes and costs of unhappiness. Here are a few points that it makes that caught our attention:

- **Mental illness** – One of the primary causes of human misery, it doesn't matter here if you adopt a medical model of distress or if you prefer another term; depression and anxiety as mental states, and also the most prevalent forms of the phenomenon, clearly exist whether you like the term 'illness' or not. Since the authors use the term, we will carry on using it here. Mental illness is a much greater determinant of deep levels of unhappiness than physical health problems, income, employment status, age, marital status or gender.

- **Emotional health experienced as a child** – A critical determinant of life satisfaction at 34, this is really no surprise to psychotherapists!

- **The cost of mental illness** – If ignored, the cost is huge for the economies of the world – in OECD countries, economic output is reduced by up to 6% as a result.

- **Much of the problem of mental illness goes untreated** – This is true of approaching half of all cases in more wealthy countries and far more in poorer ones.

- **Most treatments are cost neutral in the medium term** – In the long term, the cost of treatment is far less than the economic benefits accrued.

- **Talk therapies** – CBT and other talk therapies produce similar recovery rates to drugs but have much lower rates of relapse.

- **Risk factors** – There are clear risk and protective factors for mental health and some of these can be directly addressed in the workplace.

Risk and Protective Factors for Mental Health

Level of determinant	Risk factors	Protective factors
Individual attributes	• Low self-esteem • Emotional immaturity • Difficulties in communicating • Medical illness, substance abuse	• Self-esteem, confidence • Ability to manage stress • Communication skills • Physical health, fitness
Social circumstances	• Loneliness, bereavement • Neglect, family conflict • Exposure to violence or abuse • Low income and poverty • Difficulties or failure at school • Work stress, unemployment	• Social support of family and friends • Good parenting and family interactions • Physical security and safety • Economic security • Scholastic achievement • Satisfaction and success at work
Environmental factors	• Poor access to basic services • Injustice and discrimination • Exposure to war or disaster	• Equality of access to basic services • Social justice, tolerance, integration • Physical security and safety

Source: World Happiness Report 2013, Table 3.3, p.48

If you look at this table carefully, at least four of the risk factors could be addressed by good workplace training and, by the same token, the organisation that you work in and the job that you do could be responsible for a great deal of misery if you don't look after yourself.

What's Happening in Your Organisation?

Good questions to ask as we close this chapter on mood are:

- Does your job, your boss, your colleagues and in general the organisation in which you work add to your self-esteem and confidence?

- What's your organisation's narrative on stress? You have picked this book up and you are reading it. Is this something that your organisation would support? If not, why not?

- Are you encouraged to develop your communication skills and in what way? We don't just mean the skills of public speaking or how to put a nice presentation together; we mean the fundamental skills that allow you to connect with other people at work.

- To what extent are you encouraged to stay fit, to eat well and to manage your alcohol intake or are none of these spoken about?

- How satisfied do you feel in your job? Does your level of personal satisfaction really matter to your employer?

If you are concluding that the answers to these questions are mostly negative, we'd suggest that no matter how hard you study what's contained in this book and other books like it, no matter how much work you do on yourself and no matter how much coaching and support you get, you will always be constrained by the culture in which you work. If this is the case and if it's viable, look for another job!

You might recall that in her first coaching session Martha was invited to reflect on what success was for her. It was the third session before she felt ready to come back to this question. There always seemed more important things to talk about and the idea of discussing what she was put on Earth to do felt a bit abstract and probably quite self-indulgent.

The question came back on the agenda when Martha's coach commented on her appearance. She looked hot, flustered and tense. When he asked her how she was feeling, Martha looked a little perplexed and then simply said 'fine'. They then talked about how Martha was getting on with her boss and if any of the techniques – like the temperature check or the action-feeling statements – were proving helpful. Martha said they were and that her relationship with her boss felt much improved, for now at least.

A comfortable silence followed. Martha's coach didn't interrupt this and eventually Martha spoke. 'A friend said to me that all coaching is life coaching by the third session', she offered. There was a touch of sadness in her voice and her coach noticed that he had a strong urge to comfort her. In turn, Martha suddenly became aware that she was glad that she had an older male coach and wondered what this meant.

The fact was that although Martha had started to talk about her life outside work at the beginning of the coaching relationship, something had stopped her returning to the subject. An image of her father flashed in front of Martha and she started to feel anxious and sad.

Again, Martha's coach asked her how she was feeling, right here and now. This time Martha looked down to her right shoe and said, 'Fed up to be honest ... I don't know why but I feel empty inside and there's no reason for this. After all, work is going well and the candidate drug that we are looking after is showing great potential in the trials. I'm even getting on better with my Director'.

Martha's coach continued to say nothing. Martha looked crestfallen. 'It's just that I'm losing touch with who I am, I think,' she said. She explained that when she had trained as a medic, it was always with the intention of going into research. She now wondered if this was what she still wanted. She loved her job but she felt somehow disconnected from the benefits of her work. She wondered what it would have felt like if she had become a GP or a surgeon.

It seemed time to talk about success. Martha admitted that the problem was that she had never really felt successful. She felt surrounded by brighter people who had greater mastery of their subject areas. In Martha's view, she was only just up to their standards and that was because of a great deal of hard work and tenacity. Much of Martha's drive seemed to stem from a sense that she was an impostor, waiting to be found out. She realised that this even spilled out into the vestiges of her social life. Other people were better looking, more fashionable, more popular and more fun – in Martha's view at least. What Martha seemed to carry around in her head was a never-ending narrative of self-criticism. This depressed her mood and took its toll on her energy levels.

Just talking about this with someone else who was interested but not judgmental seemed to help. Martha noticed that her breathing had slowed down and that she was sitting more comfortably in her chair. She had moved back in her seat and was no longer in her starting-blocks position. She wanted to talk more ...

Top Tips for Managing Mood

- Notice how you tend to filter incoming information.
- Pay attention to the pattern of your thoughts. Keep a journal to help you with this.
- Learn to recognise your emotional triggers. We all have 'hot buttons'.
- Practise mindfulness and learn to meditate.
- Try anchoring and experiment with this approach.
- Complete the *i-resilience* questionnaire.
- Consider what help and resources are available to you in your organisation.

Don't forget – there's more information for each tip in **Part 2** of this book (see pages 241–254) and online at **www.sane.works**

'Don't aim at success. The more you aim at it and make it a target, the more you are going to miss it. For success, like happiness, cannot be pursued; it must ensue, and it only does so as the unintended side effect of one's personal dedication to a cause greater than oneself or as the by-product of one's surrender to a person other than oneself. Happiness must happen, and the same holds for success: you have to let it happen by not caring about it. I want you to listen to what your conscience commands you to do and go on to carry it out to the best of your knowledge. Then you will live to see that in the long-run – in the long-run, I say! – success will follow you precisely because you had forgotten to think about it.'

– Viktor E. Frankl –

Part 1

Knowledge is everywhere! (Photo by DF)

Staying sane in business is much easier if you get some help when you need it. There are lots of sources of potential informal support. Maybe you have a great boss, some good friends at work or a fantastic HR team. But imagine you need more. What are the options? Engage a coach? Talk to an Employee Assistance Programme (EAP) adviser? Maybe even get some life coaching, counselling or therapy outside work, either privately or through your GP.

The mistake that some people make is that they wait until there's a pressing problem before they look for help. Would you wait until the wheels were dropping off your car before you took it into a garage, or would morbid obesity be your only cue to join your local gym?

Of course it's not easy to exercise choice when you are upset and feeling vulnerable. As athletes will tell you, you need to drink before you are thirsty; in other words, prevention is better than cure and working with a good coach or therapist shouldn't be seen as a sign of weakness or indulgence.

There's no criticism intended in our comments. After all, to some extent the systems we find ourselves in are to blame. You probably won't get much of a hearing from a UK family doctor if you pop along and tell him or her that you have a touch of existential angst or that you'd just like a mental spring clean! Something needs to be wrong before you get much out of the medical model and sadly there still seems to be a stigma that is associated with mental distress – whether it's severe enough to be labelled an illness or whether it's simply a problem with living in the world. The same applies to coaching: it's surprising how many tears are shed in coaching and how the challenge that our clients present with is rarely the issue that they want to talk about after a couple of coaching sessions. We can see why psychologist Rob Briner has called coaching 'stigma-free therapy'!

Choosing Someone to Help

OK, say that you do decide that some coaching or psychotherapy is for you, then where do you start? There are a bewildering number of service providers out there. There are different schools of thought, multiple governing bodies and by no means one set of professional standards.

We don't advocate any one approach over another – and that goes for therapy or coaching; we think the debate about the difference between the two is pretty sterile anyway. What we are bothered about is helping you find something that works for you and gives you the chance of becoming the best version of you that is possible. Both of the authors of this book coach and we recognise that we do it in very different ways. We share common values and we recognise similar ethical frameworks, but who we are and how we practise will feel different to you as a client. If you worked with us, you would notice this and you would probably have a preference.

Here's our guide to help you find the right type of support for you. Whilst this is method agnostic, there are some pointers to leading organisations in Part 2 of this book. There are no top tips in this chapter, by the way, as the whole chapter is really a set of tips. For the sake of brevity and because this book is primarily aimed at you in business, we will mostly use the word 'coach' to cover any skilled helper – whether that's a coach, counsellor, therapist or psychologist.

In some ways, the following points may sound rather simple. That's true but it doesn't mean that they aren't important. Getting help can feel like a big step and getting the right help is critical, so ask your coach how they work and if it's not the right approach for you, then keep shopping around.

Reputation

Looking for someone to work with is a bit like looking for a plumber! Ask around. Do any work colleagues or friends have recommendations? You will soon discover that people are happier to tell you about their experiences of coaching than of therapy. Pay particular attention to the circumstances in which a coach was effective. Just because someone is great helping a client get over a fear of public speaking, it doesn't immediately follow that they will be as effective with a different problem, a different person or in a different place.

Most accreditation is based in part on hours of experience. Ask about this and also ask about the number of clients that the coach has had who sound like you. See if there are references to back up their work and, if you are looking for tangible results, don't be afraid to ask if the coach has achieved them. Don't hold back from asking about failures either. We all have them!

Chemistry

It has long been recognised that over half of the effectiveness of any coaching or therapeutic intervention is down to the relationship between the two parties. It's critical that you meet any potential helper and get a sense of what it's like being with them. Do you warm to them and could you trust them? Coaching and therapy are peculiarly intimate acts; there are few other human encounters that involve as much openness and potential vulnerability.

There's also something else that happens, called transference. When you work with a therapist or coach, feelings will arise in you that are not the direct result of the here-and-now. Some of your past will come alive and this will impact on the way your coach is with you. A properly trained coach is aware of this and uses it as part of the process of working with you. Say your coach feels a strong sense of wanting to nurture you and protect you. This might arise even when you feel no conscious desire to be looked after. The coach then becomes curious about their response to you (or their countertransference to give it its proper name) and wonders if there is a request being made from you, which is real but outside of your conscious awareness. Helping relationships swim in a sea of transference, so ask about whether it features in your coach's thinking.

Most coaches and therapists offer a free initial meeting. This is designed in part to check out the chemistry.

Tools and Techniques

If you are looking to learn new life skills, you will find a coach who works in a very structured way appealing; if you'd rather be in a supportive relationship with someone and use the time to think, you might find techniques a bit intrusive. All helpers use some techniques and most will stress the importance of starting with a coaching or therapeutic contract. This contract gives a shape to what you are working on.

If you like working at the level of thought, tools and techniques can be very helpful and they can give you a sense of mastery. You could also think of learning techniques as giving you markers along the way as you move towards your goal. In both therapy and coaching, techniques such as CBT and NLP offer a number of useful tools.

One thing to be aware of here is whether you are using tools as a proxy for something else. Some development through coaching, and most through psychotherapy, involves being aware of your feelings, what they are telling you and how to work with them, hence the previous chapter. If you keep pushing your feelings away by grappling with *technique*, when you would be better exploring them, you will limit your own development.

Humour

This is a very individual thing. Humour can relieve tension, build bridges and alliances; it can also be annoying and inappropriate. If you need to be contacted through banter, then a very serious and earnest coach may not work for you. On the other hand, if you are very upset and need a lot of kind reassurance or if you feel the pressing need to get down to business straight away, you could find humour to be trivial, unwelcome and a barrier. If you have a genuine need for some lightness in the way you interact with others – and proving this isn't being used as a veneer to cover something else – there's nothing in the rule book that says coaching or therapy has to be deadly solemn all the time.

Past versus Present

Some people argue that coaching is about looking forwards and therapy is about looking backwards. This is far too much of a simplification for our taste but we can see the value in coaching addressing the question 'where do I go from here?' and therapy helping answer 'how did I get here?' It's really a blend of the two in most cases: you want to get somewhere but there's something holding you back. Deciding to get help often arises from a sense of being stuck.

If you think or feel that there's something in your past that's unsettling you, then selecting a coach who can support you in gently examining this is a good idea. Examining material that has not been looked at for a long time and is surrounded by your defence mechanisms takes time, skill and patience. If you are looking specifically for a coach, this is one place where a dual-qualified coach-therapist could be ideal. Because this is such a sensitive area, it's perfectly appropriate to ask about the amount of work that your coach/therapist has done on themselves. How much personal therapy or coaching have they had and very importantly are they in supervision?

Of course, you might not feel this way and your preference could be to focus on what's happening now and the plans you have for the future. If this is the case for you, just be careful with denial. It may be that you haven't fully dealt with your emotional baggage and even though your positive intention to make the most of the future is laudable, there will always be something that seems to pull you backwards. Many schools of therapy have the idea of 'script' or 'schema' – a sort of plan that you write for yourself early on. What can be particularly pernicious about a script is that it can significantly limit the choices you make without you realising it.

Let's say, for example, that your coaching contract is for you to explore being more socially outgoing so you meet more people and form a wider range of meaningful relationships. Perhaps you are lonely in your private life or you find it hard to influence people to do things at work. Working on technique might be great but if you have a script that sits behind the scenes which says that you are an unlikable person who deserves to be unhappy, then you are likely to sabotage your own best efforts. An unexamined script acts like a set of brakes and, worse still, compels you to set up situations where it can be proved right. These situations are psychological games and they have a nasty habit of making you feel worse and not better. Looking backwards at the patterns in your life can, therefore, be really helpful and a good coach should be able to assist you in working through things that might be holding you back.

Being Challenged

You might really enjoy being challenged and stretched. Your idea of help could be like a mental boot camp and, if this is the case, you need to work with a coach who is happy to give you a push and to hold you to account for progress. A couple of notes of caution, though. Firstly, your coach is not there to drive the agenda. Don't expect a good outcome from coaching or therapy if you turn up and expect someone else to do all the hard work! Secondly, if you see your coach as a substitute parent (and there's nothing wrong with this) be aware that the ultimate goal of therapy or coaching is your autonomy: you as an integrated adult, free from material that isn't yours and fully accepting of all that you are. Eventually your new 'parent' will cease to be this figure and you will need to stand on your own two feet. The very thought of this loss might be quite disturbing to you.

Feelings, Thoughts and Behaviours

We all have a preference to be 'contacted' in different ways. Some years ago a therapist called Paul Ware put a lot of thought into this. He noticed that some ways of relating to clients were significantly more effective than others.

A lot of this is down to how our personalities have adapted to the challenges of growing up. Have a think about how you are under pressure and how you maintain feeling good. What are your OK-if statements?

Remember, these are your psychological drivers. Go back and reread Chapters 1 and 2 if you need to.

If you are driven to please people, working with a helper who tries to contact you by talking about your behaviour could be disturbing. After all, aren't you already doing everything that you can to keep people happy? It's not good to hear that this isn't the case. For you, it would be better to talk about your feelings and really explore them before moving on to your thoughts. Stay off talking about behaviours as this isn't going to help – at first anyway.

The same applies if you have a driver that compels you to be perfect. Again, you don't need reminding of any mistakes. It would be better, if you have this driver, to talk about your thoughts and then to go onto your feelings. Again, examining behaviours isn't as good in this case.

Homework

Some coaches set a lot of homework. The very least you should expect is to be invited to reflect on the experience you have between sessions. A lot of personal development is about increasing your awareness of thoughts and feelings. It's generally not about forcing through change, as change that is forced rarely sticks. You could be asked to keep a reflective journal, to note down events that happen to you between sessions or even to expose yourself to learning by carefully trying out something new.

Ask about the amount of homework that you will be given between sessions and consider if this feels appropriate. Is it enough or could it feel too much? Are you committed to it?

Connection

Next comes the question of connection. Coaching and therapy are based not so much on technique as on relationships. How will you manage the relationship between sessions? Some helpers have a very clear boundary. They don't allow any contact between sessions. Others are comfortable, within reason, to be emailed with your thoughts (this particularly applies to coaching) and some are even OK with texts. We live in a much more immediate and connected world than we used to. It's best if you can get the ground rules on between-session contacting clear at the start, otherwise they are a potential cause of friction and upset. Don't be shy about asking this question up front and if you feel your needs changing as your coaching or therapy progresses, then talk about it.

Strengths-Based Work

Some while ago, a new branch of psychology started to emerge and this tends to focus much more on what you are good at than where you find difficulties in life and work. This is often called positive psychology.

If this appeals to you, you might be interested in working with a coach who is interested in this school of thought and you might like to do some reading around the subject or try a couple of strengths-based assessments before you start.

Supervision and Transference

Whilst it's a bit of a misleading title in some ways, the idea of supervision is really important. Your coach or therapist's supervisor is not a person who stands over their work and passes judgement on its quality as much as someone who can be used as a sounding board. Supervision conversations do often involve a discussion on technique but, more importantly, they address what's happening personally for your coach as they work with you.

One area of frequent attention is ownership of material. You are going to say things in coaching or therapy that invoke feelings in your coach. The trick with feelings in these types of relationships is to work out whether they belong to you, belong to your coach or arise between the two of you. Are they part of the present or the past and if they are part of the past, whose past is it? If it's yours and you are replaying an experience that is troubling and holding you back, this could be really useful.

Let's say, for example, that you start coaching because you want to be better at networking. You have the motivation and you are aware of some of the skills of networking but, much to your frustration, you keep stalling. You approach coaching in the hope that you'll learn some new techniques but during the third session you start to worry that your coach isn't interested or that you are a burden to them. At the same time, your coach feels a strong urge to look after you, to comfort you and to make things better. This all sounds a bit odd. After all, weren't you just looking for some help in learning how to improve your networking skills?

One choice here would be to ignore these feelings as unhelpful noise in the system or to act on them at a superficial level. This might involve you quitting the current coaching relationship and finding another. Your conclusion might have been that the coach wasn't the right one for you and that you should be working with someone who is better with the task in hand. Suppose, instead, you worked directly with the feelings? Let's say your coach took his feelings to his supervisor and when he discussed them it became clear that they were of importance and that they could be very enlightening. Having had the feelings and checked them out in supervision, he now tells you how he feels. You, in turn, talk about how you feel. Together you conclude that what was being felt but not said by you was a fear of rejection and when you trace this back, you locate its origins. Your coach's response to your unspoken fears was to want to nurture and support you.

What might have become clear in this scenario is that building your networking skills will only ever be of limited use until you work through your own underlying feelings about being rejected and abandoned. That, more than anything else, is the source of the blockage. What you were doing in coaching was re-exploring a pattern of thoughts and feelings from your past and once this has been done in an open, supportive and insightful way, it's interesting to see how much less potent these feelings can be.

If you want a quick way of exploring how your coach works in this respect, simply ask them about transference, because that's what we are technically talking about here. Transference is defined as transferring feelings, attitudes, beliefs and patterns of thought that were appropriate to one place and time in the past to an analogous situation in the present. This is done out of conscious awareness.

If your would-be coach looks blank or dismisses your enquiry, it will be an indication that they don't work this way. As we said at the start, in our view there are no wrongs and rights; no one style of coaching or therapy that is really better than the others, but there are styles that might better suit you than others. So, if you can't quite put your finger on what the problem is or if you think there's a kind of internal impasse happening for you, you might just want to seek out a helper who is skilled at working with transference.

Relationships

We discussed above that different styles suit different people and nowhere is this truer than when you consider your preference for being challenged and confronted. If you entered coaching or therapy with a clear desire to be pushed and given clear feedback when you haven't met the objectives that you have set for yourself, then you need to find a coach who is prepared to do this. Some coaches and therapists have a naturally sharper style than others! Of course, if your life experience has been dominated by not being heard, recognised or appreciated, immediate challenge may not be welcomed and may just set off all the negative feelings in you that you are finding it hard to deal with.

Before you decide on who is best placed to support you, have a think about your motives. A healthy coaching or therapeutic relationship should be a partnership of equals but the responsibility for change in your life will always be with you. Entering a helping relationship in the hope that someone will tell you what to do is doomed to failure. Having said that, if you are looking for a nudge or a shared perspective, it can be really annoying if your helper just reflects back what you have said or simply asks you what you are feeling. Over half of the effectiveness in therapy and coaching is down to the relationship you have with the person you have chosen to help you and that relationship will develop over time.

You should feel listened to, supported and encouraged and the feelings that you bring should be welcomed and accepted. Some writers talk about non-judgement and we'd agree with that. Coaching and therapy is no place to feel judged but that doesn't mean you won't feel all sorts of other feelings as you peel back the layers of your personal onion skin.

A good coach provides a safe space in which to digest the material that has been giving you psychological indigestion. If you aren't prepared to feel your feelings in coaching and therapy it could be that you have chosen the wrong person to work with. If this type of support is going to be of any lasting use to you, it has to operate well beyond the level of thinking. If in some way, you haven't yet had your emotional needs met, it's likely that you will set up all sorts of games in order to do so. Many of these could leave you confused and asking why did I do that? A good coach or therapist can help you explore the patterns of behaviour that you'd like to change and understand them better. Once discussed, explored and understood in a supportive but challenging environment where their emotional impact can be felt without the fear of you being overwhelmed, they tend to dissipate and lose their grip over you.

Levels of Therapeutic Relationship

If you are going to engage in a coaching or therapeutic relationship, you are likely to become curious about your coach. You'll wonder what their story is, how they became the person they are and what personal demons they might have dealt with in their lives. You might feel inclined to ask …

The fact is that coaches and therapists operate in different ways – some favour a different level of intimacy than others and some vary the level of intimacy according to the needs of the client. Indeed, it has been argued that in therapy at least, there are three modes of operating. Back in 2000, a US therapist called Martha Stark came up with the idea that these types of relationships could be one-person, one-and-a-half-person or two-person. She didn't necessarily claim that one mode is better than another but at different times and for different issues it might be that one suits you better than the rest.

- **One-person relationship** – According to Stark, this is all about interpretation. The coach or therapist is focused on what's happening in the world of the client with the goal of developing insight and understanding. You could argue that this is what classical psychoanalysis was all about. Hence the term 'analyst: one who analyses and comes to conclusions'. There's a lot to be said for this mode of operating and without any great attachment to their coach or therapist, clients can extract a lot of value from simply understanding themselves better.

- **One-and-a-half person relationship** – This curiously named mode differs in that the coach or therapist explores the internal world of the client by being empathic and by attuning to the client's needs. At the root of all humanistic approaches to working with clients is the idea of shared experience of the world, of a client being understood and of a relationship that is free of judgement. If your coach works at the level of empathy, this could help you with things that are being felt at the edge of conscious awareness but that are difficult to explore directly.

- **Two-person mode** – Probably the most intimate way of working, this directly uses the relationship between you and your coach or therapist as a means of making progress. The idea is that within clear boundaries and in a safe place, the dynamics of your past relationships are explored by allowing them to play out in the relationship you have with your helper. In this type of work, your coach does not merely enter your world and seek to understand you but they become part of your world and together you co-create material that is used for your personal growth and development.

Let's take an example. Let's say you enter into coaching because, like Martha, you are having a difficult relationship with your boss. You would like to get on better with her but every encounter seems to end the same way with you feeling bad. A one-person approach could be to explore this in detail and to locate a time in your past where you first felt like this. You realise that the pattern is familiar and that your boss always reminds you of a difficult relationship with an older sibling. A one-and-a-half-person approach might be where your coach notices your feelings of hurt, shame and anger and works directly with these feelings and in a two-person approach you transfer the face of your sibling onto your coach and the relationship between you plays out as if your coach really is your sibling.

Silence

Some coaches and therapists use silence a lot. There's a whole approach to coaching by Nancy Kline that is based on Time to Think. Something to consider is how comfortable you are with silence and, for that matter, how comfortable your coach is too. Our view is that silence and a space to collect and digest your thoughts and feelings are often of great value in coaching and therapy. That said, we feel that silence should never be used as a weapon and that you shouldn't feel intimidated by it. Going right back to Chapter 1, at the simplest level, the appetite for silence will differ between introverts and extroverts. Introverts really welcome the uninterrupted space, and need someone to work with who will provide this. Extroverts, on the other hand, tend to think by talking and can find what feels like a long period of silence disconcerting. Try to select a coach who matches your preference.

The Life Outside

Coaching and therapy are not the only ways of achieving personal growth. There are many routes to staying sane in business and coming at the challenge from different angles can be very helpful.

Whilst your coach or therapist can't be skilled in everything, it can be very helpful if they are able and willing to point you in the right direction or at least be supportive of other ways of looking after yourself.

After all, if you regularly drink to excess, you smoke, your diet consists of anything that you can grab as you dash from one place to another and your idea of exercise is running a bath, you can't really expect to operate at an optimum level! A coach who fails to mention any of this is, in our opinion, only doing half the job.

Here are some things that might be talked about in a coaching or therapy session that aren't just about thoughts, feelings and beliefs.

Diet

It's true that you are what you eat. If you are not eating well, you will significantly decrease your personal resilience. Your immune response, your energy and your mood all to some extent depend on the quality of your nutrition. The same applies to your level of hydration. Some coaches and therapists have a particular interest in this area or you might consider taking separate nutritional advice. You might talk about any of the following. If you are not talking about them in your coaching or therapy, and they are a problem, you risk hampering your progress.

- **Caffeine** – Many of us love a decent coffee. Most people know caffeine is a stimulant. But overdo it and you will end up with too much adrenalin in your system and this can ruin your sleep, make you generally nervous and skittish and give you high blood pressure. If you need a double espresso just to keep awake, perhaps you need to ask yourself why. It's not just coffee of course – many carbonated drinks contain just as much caffeine, if not more.

- **Sugar** – This is one product we can all do without and indeed we used to. The trouble is that the stuff is everywhere and it's not always labelled. Sugar in the form of added sucrose makes food taste good but it has no nutritional value whatsoever. All that sucrose does is cause your pancreas to overwork and makes you susceptible to diabetes.

- **Nutrition** – There's a lot of nonsense spoken about diet and nutrition. The simple truth is that it's all about balance. If you are going to stay mentally healthy, you need sufficient A, B and C vitamins, protein and essential minerals like magnesium. You already know if your diet is balanced so it's best to face up to it. You cannot be at your best just eating processed food laced with fat, sugar and salt and skipping on fresh fruit and vegetables. Sorry, but it's just not possible!

- **Alcohol** – Potentially beneficial in moderation, alcohol is a euphoric and there's even evidence that some consumption of red wine has cardio-vascular benefits. If you aren't naturally outgoing, alcohol can be a wonderful social lubricant. But it's not moderate consumption of alcohol that's the problem and it's not even the excess that you might indulge in at the office party. Alcohol becomes an issue when you repeatedly take it to stop you feeling something. Self-medication is rarely a good idea.

Lifestyle

Alongside diet come the lifestyle choices you make. We doubt if there is anything here that you have not heard before, but that doesn't make the information any less crucial. Again, all of these could feature in a coaching relationship designed to preserve business sanity!

- **Smoking** – The risks are known. There's really hardly anything to say about this one...

- **Drugs** – Whether you are hyping yourself up, attempting to calm yourself down and whether your choice of drugs is over the counter, on prescription or via more nefarious means, the same principle applies as to alcohol: you are using the drugs to alter the way you feel and probably not to feel something that is distressing you. We could fill a book with observations about drugs and we accept that the debate is a complex one. The fact remains that many of the clients we see in therapy cite drugs of one kind or another as part of their problems.

- **Exercise** – This has been shown to be at least as effective as mild doses of anti-depressants, plus it has a beneficial effect on sleep. We mentioned our friend Clive, who was a motivational speaker. Clive concluded he was depressed and one way out of his mental state, he discovered, was to move. Coining the phrase that 'emotion follows motion', he noticed that if he moved, the remote control of his television out of reach he had to get up to change the channel. Catching the momentum of his walk across his living room, he reasoned that whilst he was on his feet, he may as well go into the kitchen and make himself a drink. Whilst he was waiting for the kettle to boil, he may as well wash the dishes. Every small movement gave him the momentum to do something else and every small task gave him a sense of accomplishment that chipped away at his sadness and gloom. So with exercise, we aren't necessarily talking about an Iron Man yomp across the moors or gruelling but ultimately unsustainable sessions in the gym: three sessions of something that makes you mildly out of breath, three times a week – that's all. A walk, a swim, a bike ride or a game of tennis. They all help.

- **Rest and recreation** – Something we all need, the word 'recreation' itself is curious and instructive. We need time offline to re-create ourselves. There are no hard-and-fast rules here and what works for one person doesn't necessarily work for another but in a hyper-connected world where the boundaries between work and home are now completely blurred, we all have to ask ourselves how we avoid existing in a state of continuous partial attention and over-stimulation. You should expect your coach or therapist to be interested in this area. They might come at it from different angles, perhaps helping you learn the technique of muscle relaxation that is so important for the relief of tension; then again they might be helping you become more creative – and that's not going to include encouraging you to spend more time on your smartphone, waiting to react to the next email. They might even point out to you that one way of achieving greater happiness is to learn a new skill. If they are really able to work with you as a whole person, expect them to say something!

- **Spirituality** – If you have a strong faith, spirituality is likely to be an important part of your identity. Working with a coach or therapist of the same faith could be very enriching. Some people mistakenly believe that all coaching and therapy is totally secular in nature. This is not true. Whilst a good coach would not judge you for your beliefs and would never impose their own beliefs upon you, it doesn't follow that spirituality has no place in the relationship. There's nothing stopping you looking for a helper from a particular religion or philosophy. All that we would suggest is that you clearly contract for this at the outset.

- **Background** – A helper with a particular kind of life experience might be what you are looking for. That's one reason to do your homework and to ask. Even so, remember that although coaching and therapy operate on a continuum from completely non-directive to directive, all coaching and therapy stops short of telling you what to do. Nevertheless, if you want to work with a therapist who has also been exposed to the commercial world, for example, (there are many who have since most psychotherapists enter the profession later in life), then that's fine. Equally, of course, it could be appealing to work with someone who sees the world in a completely different way to you. What are important are the twin concerns of challenge and connection. Challenge is all about the ability of your helper to increase your level of choice and to help you think about possible courses of action that don't feel open to you at the moment. Connection is more about a sense of being understood, appreciated and recognised for who you are.

Finding a Coach or Therapist

As we mentioned above, one of the best ways to find a coach or therapist is to ask other people. In this respect, helping professions are no different from any others: reputation counts. If you don't know anyone to ask or if asking doesn't feel comfortable, there are many places to look on the web. We have included a few starting points in Part 2 of this book (see page 256). For the most part, coaching and therapy are unregulated professions. Over time, this could well change and there are already some very helpful voluntary registers that are some assurance of a level of quality, adherence to a set of ethical standards and commitment to continuous professional development.

Our advice is tread carefully though not over-cautiously and pay a lot of attention to your intuitive responses when assessing a would-be coach. Also be practical. Coaching and therapy require regular investments of time and effort. Having a coach who practises a long way away and who takes a great deal of time and effort to visit is just another barrier that you don't need. Try and find the best person for you who is able to provide support when you need it and without an enormous journey.

Understanding the Process of Personal Change

Change is a slow process. The beliefs that you have, the ways you interact with others, and the ways you respond to stress and pressure have all developed to protect you. Even if they are unhelpful or perhaps even destructive now, they exist because at some point in your life they kept you feeling safe and secure. The problem with these patterns of thinking, feeling and behaving is that they can tend to stick around beyond the point that they're useful.

This is to be expected. It is normal and completely understandable for these ways of thinking, feeling and interacting with others to take a while to 'shift'. It's really not normal to change abruptly and if you see people do this, the chances are that before long they will have slipped back to their old ways. Sustainable change requires patience and if you feel rushed along by coaching or therapy, we think this should sound an alarm bell.

Psychologists have been thinking about personal change for a long time. Some of the most insightful work has come from studying addiction.

A useful way to think about change is offered by Prochaska and Di-Clemente (1984), who broke down the change process into five steps.

- **Pre-contemplation** – This is the 'blissfully unaware' stage of the change process. If you are in this stage, you are not aware of the need to change and you are often unaware of the impact of the issue in question on your day-to-day life. Of course, other people might be, and it may be from them that the need to change starts to be discussed. Medically, something like high blood pressure is a good comparison. Hypertension doesn't always have symptoms and the first you know of it is when you have a routine examination. This is the first stage of the change process.

- **Contemplation** – At this stage, you have become aware of the problem requiring attention. You will be conscious of the impact that this issue is having on your day-to-day life but you will not yet be taking any steps to make changes. This is often quite an uncomfortable place to be. You know you need to do something but either you haven't really started or you aren't sure where to start. It is the second stage of the change process.

- **Preparation** – At this point, you are taking steps to prepare yourself for change. This may involve psychological preparations (considering your emotional needs in readiness for making something happen, such as seeking social and/or emotional support from friends) and practical preparations (taking steps to accommodate the new change into your life). It is the third stage of the change process and it's often the one that's rushed. Having acknowledged that something needs to happen, you itch to get started. Let's say you wanted to do a 60-kilometre charity bike ride. Would you leap on a new bike and just do it, having not really ridden once since the day you discarded your stabilisers, or would you carefully embark on a training programme to get you to the right level of fitness? On the whole, this is the stage where we fail to look before we leap, try something either with initial gusto that quickly fades away or kick off in an entirely half-hearted manner!

Modern life implores us to hurry up. Expect an effective coach to encourage you to slow down! Also, beware of negative goals. Years of research has shown that negative goals don't work. So don't prepare to *lose* weight, *stop* smoking, worry *less* or *not* lose your temper in the office. If you have a young child you already know this to be true. If you ask them not to spill something on your carpet, have you noticed what happens? If you want a positive change, set a positive goal. Imagine being slim and fit, having the money you used to spend on cigarettes, or attaining a Zen-like calmness in the office. Your unconscious processing is just like that small child. Bring its attention to what you don't want and what you don't want is exactly what will happen! Bring its attention to what you do want and let it do its work offline.

- **Action** – At this point, you are enacting the change you have prepared for. The more that you have prepared and envisioned the positive and desirable end state, the more likely it is that this stage will be a success. The key thing that sets this stage apart from the others is that at this stage, there really will be psychological and/or practical changes occurring in your life. What you are working on will be visible to you and others. This is the fourth stage and what's often forgotten is that all change at some level includes loss. Making any choice requires you to let go of another option and we can all overlook this. It's what we let go of that sometimes bothers us as we don't realise the value of that thing until it has gone.

Let's say that you have a wedding coming up and you'd really like to wear some clothes that don't fit you at the moment. Surveying your expanded midriff, you decide to take action: less food and more exercise for a month. You make some sensible plans and you draw up a diet sheet and find your gym card that has been languishing in a kitchen drawer. It's all going well but then the horrible realisation hits you that Friday night is the time you love to meet your friends in the pub and then visit your favourite Indian restaurant. This all feels a bit too calorific, so you make your excuses and stay home. Lonely and bored, it's not long before you start nibbling on snacks! Your plan was fine but you forgot to take into account something that you were going to have to let go of and that was the joy of social contact.

- **Maintenance** – At this stage, you have taken the initial steps to make the change, and you are now seeking to maintain that change for the longer term. This involves you integrating the change into your life in a way that is sustainable for the future. This is the final stage of the change process and you might argue the most important. How many of you reading this book have yo-yo dieted for example? In many ways, problems that might occur at this stage are extensions of the action stage. Your social group plays a huge role here too. Imagine that you have cut back a great deal on what you are drinking. Summer has come and gone and you enjoyed many weeks of sobriety in the sun. Now it's the run up to Christmas. The invites for the office parties come in and your role in past years has been chief merrymaker. Your alcohol-fuelled antics have become legendary and your work friends can't wait for this year's instalment. Here's the test of your resolve. Stick with the new way of being and run the risk of social exclusion or go along with the pack ... it's only a few nights out after all ...

- **Relapse** – This word often brings a feeling of dread, but is actually entirely expected and normal. When making a change, from time to time you will slip back into old habits, ways of thinking, behaving and living your life – or at least you will be very tempted to. This can involve relapse to any of the above stages, but is totally normal. The important thing is to consider that this doesn't always mean 'going back to square one'. Consider what caused the slip, how you can avoid that in future, and how you can restart the change process. We talked about mindfulness earlier in the book. If you start meditating, you will find it very difficult to stop your mind wandering at first but that's no reason to give up. Stick with it.

Enjoy the Journey

Good luck with finding the right person to help you. They are out there. Shop around and sample a few. Enjoy the journey as much as the destination. There's no weakness in seeking support; quite the opposite – it's a mark of strength.

We hope this short book has been helpful. We suspect that our lives are much the same as yours and we don't claim to have all of the answers. What we have shared are simply a few pointers along the way. Dip into the Part 2 of this book and go to **www.sane.works** Let us know what you think and please, please add to the debate by posting your thoughts and comments. We all have a part to play in helping each other stay sane in business!

In the end we make no special claims. It's our belief that all that is truly useful about how to stay happy, productive and mentally healthy is already known, though maybe not always accepted. In fact, it has been known for a very long time. All of us are simply re-discovering what we know to be the truth, each successive generation doing so in their own language and frequently believing that they are on to something new!

This was written in 1927 but it feels so timeless that it was mistakenly thought to have been written centuries ago!

Go placidly amid the noise and haste, and remember what peace there may be in silence. As far as possible without surrender be on good terms with all persons.

Speak your truth quietly and clearly; and listen to others, even the dull and the ignorant; they too have their story.

Avoid loud and aggressive persons, they are vexations to the spirit. If you compare yourself with others, you may become vain and bitter; for always there will be greater and lesser persons than yourself.

Enjoy your achievements as well as your plans. Keep interested in your own career, however humble; it is a real possession in the changing fortunes of time.

Exercise caution in your business affairs; for the world is full of trickery. But let this not blind you to what virtue there is; many persons strive for high ideals; and everywhere life is full of heroism.

Be yourself. Especially, do not feign affection. Neither be cynical about love; for in the face of all aridity and disenchantment it is as perennial as the grass.

Take kindly the counsel of the years, gracefully surrendering the things of youth.

Nurture strength of spirit to shield you in sudden misfortune. But do not distress yourself with dark imaginings. Many fears are born of fatigue and loneliness.

Beyond a wholesome discipline, be gentle with yourself. You are a child of the universe, no less than the trees and the stars; you have a right to be here. And whether or not it is clear to you, no doubt the universe is unfolding as it should.

Therefore be at peace with God, whatever you conceive Him to be, and whatever your labors and aspirations, in the noisy confusion of life keep peace with your soul. With all its sham, drudgery, and broken dreams, it is still a beautiful world. Be cheerful. Strive to be happy.

Max Ehrmann, 'Desiderata' (1872–1945)

Be all that you are. (Photo by DF)

Part 2

This section of the book is composed of practical suggestions, tools and techniques. It follows on from the Top Tips that conclude each chapter. It also works hand in hand with our web-based resources at **www.sane.works** Some things are better on the net!

We all develop in different ways, so we have suggested three distinct modes of taking action. Each mode will have a different level of appeal to you depending on how you like to learn, how much time you have and probably what mood you are in. Pick and choose.

 See – is about finding out more. We have listed things to read but it could also be a play, a film or a physical place to visit. It could also be a book, a YouTube clip or a lecture.

 Think – is all about reflection. Eyes closed on a train, in the bath, walking the dog ... it doesn't matter where. Don't forget, though, to note down the results of your thoughts. Don't let them drift away.

 Do – is an activity. We can learn a lot by doing. We learn even more if we reflect on what we have done. If you undertake an activity, do it just for you; there's nobody more important to please.

By the way, you can download a full-sized version of each table in this part of the book by visiting **www.sane.works** Sometimes it's nice to print things off and scribble on them!

Personal Narrative

 Do

Close your eyes and imagine you are watching a film about yourself.

- How did it start?
- What is happening at this moment in time?

Move forward to the imagined end.

- What are people saying about you? What you stood for; what you lived for?
- What did your actions say about you as a person?
- What did your actions say about what you valued?
- Do these implied values seem consistent with what you actually value?
- If any of them are inconsistent, which one makes you feel the most uncomfortable?
- How do you want the film to end? Are there any changes you want to make?
- What actions do you need to take to stay well and create the right ending for you both professionally and personally?

 See

Gerhardt, S., (2004). *Why Love Matters*. Routledge.

Greenfield, S., (2000). *The Private Life of the Brain*. Penguin.

Perry, P., (2012). *How to Stay Sane*. Macmillan.

Steiner, C., (1974). *Scripts People Live*. Grove Press.

Meaning and Values

 Think

Ponder these big questions.

- What things give you a sense of meaning in life?
- What makes you feel challenged?
- What activities or interests make you lose track of time?
- What makes you happy? (For example, activities, people, events, roles, hobbies.)
- Whose happiness is intertwined with yours?
- Who do you currently feel responsible for?
- Who do you want to feel responsible for?
- What makes you feel great about yourself?
- What are your innermost values?
- What do you believe in?
- What do you aspire to achieve?
- What does success mean for you?
- If you could change one thing about your life, what would it be?
- If you had more hours in the day what would you do?
- If you did volunteering what might you do?
- If you could have any career what would it be?

If nobody ever heard your values, and only you knew them, what would you say they were?

- How much are your values about what you want, and how much of them is what other people want from you?
- If other people are influencing your values, then what's the impact?
- How would you be behaving if you were living consistently with these values?

- Who would you be with?
- Where would you be?
- What would you be doing?
- What would you be thinking – about yourself, about your future, about other people?
- What would the impact of those thoughts be on your happiness?
- What is preventing you from behaving in that way?
- What can you do to start behaving in a way that is consistent with these value(s)?

 ## See

Aronson, E., (1997). Back to the Future: Retrospective review of Leon Festinger's 'A theory of cognitive dissonance'. *The American Journal of Psychology*, 110, pp. 127–137.

Aronson, E., Chase, T., Helmreich, R., & Ruhnke, R., (1974). A two-factor theory of dissonance reduction: The effect of feeling stupid or feeling awful on opinion change. *International Journal for Research and Communication*, 3, pp. 59–74.

Batten, S. J., (2011). *Essentials of Acceptance and Commitment Therapy*. Sage: London.

Booker, C., (2004). *The Seven Basic Plots*. Continuum.

Carr, A., (2011). *Positive Psychology*. Routledge.

Dilts, R. & Gilligan, S., (2009). *The Hero's Journey*. Crown House Publishing.

O'Connor, J., (2001). *NLP Workbook*. Element.

Festinger, L., (1957). *A Theory of Cognitive Dissonance*. Evanston, IL: Row, Peterson.

Frankl, V., (1946). *Man's Search for Meaning*. Random House.

Harris, R., (2009). *ACT Made Simple: A Quick-Start Guide to ACT Basics and Beyond.* Oakland, CA: New Harbinger Publications Inc.

Motivation

 Think

Complete this table to explore what sorts of factors impact your level of motivation.

Factors affecting motivation

	Think of a time when you felt very *motivated* at work. Now reflect on the questions below in relation to your raised level of motivation.	Describe a time when you felt very *de-motivated* at work. Now reflect on the questions below in terms of your reduced level of motivation.
What were you working on?		
What skills were you using?		
Where were you working?		
What was the environment like?		
Who else was involved?		

What was interesting?		
How was the workload?		
How much time was involved?		
How much attention did you pay to your wellbeing during this time?		
What did it feel like to be that motivated/de-motivated?		
How did it affect your mood?		
What impact did your mood have on your colleagues?		
What impact did your mood have on other people outside work?		
What changed in the way you related to others?		

	Think of a time when you felt very *motivated* at work. Now reflect on the questions below in relation to your raised level of motivation.	Describe a time when you felt very *de-motivated* at work. Now reflect on the questions below in terms of your reduced level of motivation.
How would other people describe you at this time?		
What feedback did you receive?		
How were you recognised for your inputs?		
How were you rewarded for your outputs?		
What did you appreciate about yourself?		
What did you learn about yourself?		

Based on the table above, what factors impact your motivation levels?

On a scale of one to ten, how would you rate your current level of motivation at work?

- What would make it a ten out of ten?
- What is the first step you will take?

See

McClelland, D., (1965). Toward a theory of motive acquisition. *American Psychologist*, 20, pp. 321–33.

 ## Do

There are a number of online psychometric questionnaires designed to assess motivators. For more information see **www.sane.works** for suggestions.

Personality

 ## Think

Reflect on the following questions.

- Describe your personality in one sentence.
- Who or what has shaped your personality?
- What do you feel proud of in relation to your personality?
- When is your personality at its finest?
- Who brings out the best in you in terms of your personality?
- What personality characteristics would you like to change?
- What feedback have you received on your personality?
- Where do you feel you can be yourself?
- In what sorts of situations or contexts do you adapt your personality?
- How does your personality change under pressure?
- What impact does your personality have on others?

Do

Gather some structured feedback on your personality. This activity can be carried out via email or face to face. A coach, manager or mentor could gather the responses or you could do it yourself. Consider the pros and cons of making the questionnaire anonymous – it is up to you! You can add in your own questions. Make sure you ask a range of different people (such as managers, peers, direct reports and clients) to ensure you obtain a rounded selection of responses.

Ask ten people:

- What was your first impression of my personality?
- How has this changed over time?
- What three words would you use to describe my personality?
- What do you appreciate about my personality?
- What is the one characteristic you would like me to change?
- How does my personality help me achieve my goals at work?
- How does it hinder me?
- How does my personality change when I am under pressure?

Collate and consolidate the responses.

- What are the themes?
- What did it confirm that you already knew about yourself?
- What did other people know about you that you did not know about yourself?
- What did you learn about yourself?
- How do you feel about any surprises?
- What other information do you need?
- What will you do differently?
- What support do you require?

Do

Draw a picture that represents your personality.

- How would you describe the picture?
- How would others describe the picture?
- What colours did you use? Why?
- How do you feel about the picture?
- How would you like to change the picture? Why?

 Do

Purchase a set of Personality Poker cards (www.personalitypoker.com).

Play this business game with your team or sort the cards as a means of self-reflection. It is one of the quickest, easiest and most entertaining personality-related tools to ever hit the business market.

- Do you delight in planning and taking action?
- Do you revel in facts and data?
- Do you crave new ideas and experiences?
- Do you feel more complete when you are around others?

In other words, are you a spade, diamond, club, or heart? These cards will help you find out!

 Do

Try out PersonaBubble (www.personabubble.com). This is a free online psychometric test from a reputable publisher and it's a great start to exploring your personality and raising self-awareness.

See

Cain, S., (2012). *Quiet: The Power of Introverts in a World That Can't Stop Talking*. Penguin. Also see her website (www.thepowerofintroverts.com) and the supporting TED talk on YouTube.

Chammorro-Premuzic, T., (2011). *Personality and Individual Differences*. BPS Blackwell.

Pendleton, D. & Furnham, A., (2012). *Leadership: All You Need to Know*. Palgrave Macmillan.

Your Skills

 Think

Ask yourself these questions to identify your skills.

1. Think about three recent, specific tasks you have completed successfully at work. What skills did you use? Think about what you did (what specific actions did you take?) to achieve those tasks. Break it down step by step for each task, from the early stages of the task to its completion. What did you learn about your skill-set?

- Outline three recent, specific people related issues you have successfully managed at work. What skills did you use? Think about what you did (i.e. what actions did you take?) to address those issues. Break it down step by step, from the early stages of the activity to its completion. What did you learn about your skill-set?

- Consider a major life event you have experienced. What skills did you use to deal with it and overcome it? What would other people say you did well if you asked them? How would you describe someone else if they did the same things you did?

- Note down ten tasks you complete on a regular basis in business. What skills, knowledge and experience do you use? What do you appreciate about the skills you have?

- What do people typically ask you for help with at work? Why do they approach you? What is it that is special about your skills?

 ## Do

Brainstorm what are you naturally good at and list your skills, abilities and gifts.

- Write each skill on a post-it.
- Cluster them into groups or themes.
- Give each group or theme a name.
- Rate yourself on each skill.
- Rate where you would like to be in order to reach your goals.
- Pick between three and five skills you would like to develop. Remember you can enhance your strengths! Maybe focus on one theme or perhaps pick one skill from each group.
- Consider whether you are cut out to develop these skills.
- What action will you take?
- When will you do it by?
- How will you ensure you stay on track?
- Who will you involve?
- What will success look and feel like?

 ## Do

Create a journal of skills used in your current role, defining what the skill is, who it is relevant to, and where, when and how you use it.

Keep the journal with you so that you are aware of alternative, realistic thoughts to the kind of self-criticism we can all experience during challenging times. It might be helpful to review this periodically to remind yourself of the skills you possess and reflect on how you demonstrate them to others.

Do

Complete a skill-based questionnaire, such as The Competence Tool Kit by Paul Whiteley and Graham Robinson (Peter Honey Publications) and look at the results. Is this the pattern that you were expecting? Can you see something different?

 Do

Create a personal SWOT analysis of your strengths, weaknesses, opportunities, threats.

Strengths – things to consider	Weaknesses – things to consider
Capabilities Unique selling points Experience, knowledge, skills, qualifications Things you enjoy Things you are good at Positive feedback you've received Personality traits	Gaps in your experience, knowledge, skills and qualifications Things you least enjoy Constructive feedback you have received Things you want to develop to be more effective in your role/career
Opportunities – things to consider	**Weaknesses – things to consider**
What will help you develop further? What support is available e.g. training, coaching or mentoring opportunities, secondments and shadowing opportunities? What networking events and conferences could you attend? What other skill development options are available? How can you leverage your strengths?	What will get in the way of your development? What are the barriers to you moving forward? Reflect on your own preferences and areas. How might these undermine your development? What qualities do you have that, if you take them to the extreme end, will be unhelpful to your development (e.g. perfectionism)?

Do

Update your CV to help you to think about your skills and experience. Have a friend, partner, supplier, customer, manager and trusted colleague from a previous workplace or (if possible) your current workplace review your CV to gain specific feedback. They may highlight relevant skills, qualities or experiences you are not aware of or may have forgotten.

Relationships

 Think

Consider the following questions:

- What is your natural style of relating to others? How does your style of relating to others show itself day to day at work?
- How do you tend to relate to new business contacts? What do you do when you want to make a particularly strong first impression?
- How do you relate to people you feel at ease with? What is it about them that evokes this feeling in you? Why do you feel comfortable with them?
- How do you relate to people you feel uncomfortable with? What is it about them that makes you feel uncomfortable? Why do you feel uncomfortable with them?
- How does your style of relating to others change when you are under pressure? Why do you take this approach? What impact does this have on those around you? What impact does it have on you?

 # Think

Reflect on the following scenarios.

- If you are in a difficult situation at work, feeling upset and/or stressed out, do you want to ask for help? How do you think other people will react if you ask for help? Will they help, will they leave you to struggle, will they attack or demean you and think negatively of you deep-down?

- Have other people done that to you before when you have asked for help? Perhaps parents, siblings, teachers at school, partners or close friends?

- How do you think that kind of prediction affects your behaviour at work? Do you actually ask for help in times of stress, or do you take some other sort of action based on what you thought would happen?

- How does that work for you? How does it leave you feeling? Do you perform better or worse as a result? What else could you do instead?

 # Think

Think about how you relate to others.

- When you were growing up, how were you encouraged to relate to others?
- Who were your main role models in this regard?
- What were the implications for you if you tried to be different?
- How has your style of relating to others changed over time?
- How does this impact how you relate to others at work?

 # See

If you wish to explore the impact of your relationship blueprints and previous experiences further, and to consider how you could manage these to improve your wellbeing and performance at work, please visit Sixth Sense Consulting Ltd. (www.sixthsenseconsulting.co.uk). We provide a range of assessment, coaching and psychotherapy services for business.

 # Do

Complete the FIRO questionnaire. There's more information on this at www.opp.com/en/tools/FIRO Explore the following questions with a FIRO qualified coach.

For each question also consider: Who? Why? What? Where? How?

Inclusion

- When do you include others?
- When do you want to include others?
- When do people include you?
- When do you want people to include you?

Control

- When do you control or influence people?
- When do you want to control or influence people?
- When do people control or influence you?
- When do you want people to control or influence you?

Openness

- When are you open with people?
- When do you want to be open with people?
- When are people open with you?
- When do you want people to be open with you?

What did you learn about your style of relating to others? What could be even better? How and when will you achieve this?

Problem Solving

 Think

Think about a recent, significant problem you have **successfully** solved at work.

Deconstructing a Problem ...

What was the problem?	
How did you feel about it?	
What did you think about it at the time?	
What was your attitude to the problem?	
What action did you take?	
What skills did you use?	
Who did you involve?	
What resources did you draw upon?	
How did you break down any barriers?	
Why did you persevere?	
What was the outcome?	
What did you learn?	
How did you celebrate your success?	

Think about another, significant problem you are **struggling** with. Imagine you have solved it like you solved the problem above. Imagine what you did.

 Do

Try this exercise derived from NLP. Consider a significant business problem you have tried to solve but where, so far, you have been unsuccessful. It needs to be one that you are motivated to address!

Now, close your eyes and pretend you are at the cinema. Imagine watching a film showing how you have tried to solve the problem up to this point. Open your eyes when you get to the present.

- How did the film start?
- What did you notice about yourself in the film?
- What would a 'fly on the wall' say about your approach to problem solving?
- What is happening at this moment in time?
- What could you do differently?

Now close your eyes again. Imagine watching a film showing you successfully solving the problem. Open your eyes when the film is finished. Reflect on the imagined end.

- What are people saying about you?
- How did you solve the problem?
- What did your actions say about you as a person?
- How do you feel about yourself?

Now reflect on your current state of play regarding the problem.

- What actions are you going to take?
- How will you break down any barriers?
- When will you do it?
- Who will you involve?

- What will success look like?
- How will you celebrate?
- What will you learn?

 # Think

Consider how your own style of problem solving may help you to be better at solving particular types of problems more than others. Perhaps you can apply your style as a strength to particular kinds of problems you work on alone, or particular aspects of problems you may work on in a team.

Ask yourself the following questions:

- What kinds of problems do you think your style would suit, or not suit?
- Think of a current problem at work, or a recent problem you've experienced. What could you do, or have done, using your strengths?
- What would that have looked like?
- How can you move forward using your strengths to solve future problems?

 # Do

There are a number of online psychometric questionnaires designed to assess your approach to problem solving. These are often called situational judgement tests. For more information see **www.sane.works**

If you wish to explore the impact of your personality and experiences more, and to consider how you may use these as strengths to improve work performance, visit www.sixthsenseconsulting.co.uk to explore the range of assessment, coaching and psychotherapy services on offer.

Reputation

 Do

Volunteer for 360° feedback if your organisation offers it. There are lots of off the shelf questionnaires available or your place of work might have a specially tailored one. Reflect on how different groups of people experience you. Does your manager see different qualities in you than your peers or the people you lead? Is this what you want?

If your organisation doesn't do 360° feedback, create your own. Here's a simple form that you could use for fast feedback. Identify a minimum of five trusted colleagues (managers, peers or direct reports) who have a very good understanding of how you work and ask them to give comprehensive, honest and fair comments against the categories listed below.

Name (optional):	
Role (optional):	
Date:	
Relationship to feedback recipient, such as peer, manager (optional):	
Please tell me about those aspects of my work that I currently do well and should continue doing in the same way.	
Please tell me about those aspects of my work that are less productive or constructive, and that I should do less of.	
Please tell me about those aspects of my work where I could develop further, where I have the potential to do well.	
Please add any other feedback.	

Collate the responses and identify the themes. Consider sharing the outputs with your coach, mentor or manager. Create an action plan to address any areas you wish to develop.

 # Think

What could you do to shrink the area of 'known to others, unknown to self' in your own Johari window? Consider the following questions.

- Consider the skills, knowledge or other expertise you need to get feedback about.
- Think through which tasks those potential areas for development are used for, and who you work with most frequently on those kinds of tasks.
- Of those people, consider who you feel most comfortable with and trust the most. It is often easiest to engage with and process feedback when it occurs in a trusting, secure relationship.
- It can be helpful to get information from various sources: for example, from colleagues who have observed your work and from those you have engaged jointly with in a project or task. This helps to shrink the 'known to others, unknown to self' area of the Johari window.
- What practical steps do you need to take to gain feedback? Consider if there are any established mechanisms in the workplace that can be used to gain feedback. There may be a mentor, colleague or manager you can talk to about getting feedback.
- Be as open and honest as you can be with your colleagues about areas you feel need development, and invite feedback about those in addition to other areas your colleagues feel are relevant to the discussion.
- What are your safety strategies? How might these strategies prevent you from seeking feedback, or negatively impact on your ability to engage with the feedback? What else could you think in this situation? What else could you do – through your behaviour – to break free from these patterns?

- How could you use mindfulness to deal with the thoughts and feelings concerning the process of feedback? Could you try to 'let go' of these thoughts and engage in the present?
- Consider letting your colleagues know at the outset of any reservations or anxieties you have about gaining feedback. This can be helpful, as then the problem is named and can be discussed and addressed with your colleagues in a way that lets you feel more relaxed and secure (consider whether you feel comfortable to do this, and whether it is practical to do so).

 Think

Play with the idea of your personal brand, exploring it through metaphor.

- If you were an **animal**, what would you be and why?
- If you were a **type of food**, what would you be and why?
- If you were a **car**, what would you be and why?
- If you were a **high-street brand**, what would you be and why?
- If you were a **celebrity**, who would you be and why?

By all means, carry on and make up your own categories!

 See

Holloway, J., (2014, 2nd ed). *Personal Branding for Brits*. Spark Ltd.

Self-Observation

 Do

Try this exercise. It is a great way to begin to contact the present moment and to make you aware of what is occurring in your body and running through your mind that you might not be aware of.

- **Be comfortable** – Pick a comfortable, fairly quiet place where you won't be disturbed. Perhaps in the car outside your home before you leave for work? Put your hands on your lap or by your sides, or wherever is most comfortable. Pick a spot on the floor and let your eyes lose focus, or close your eyes, whichever is most comfortable.

- **Hearing** – Begin to relax by just noticing all of the sounds around you. Give yourself permission to suspend your judgment of the sounds. They are not good or bad, they are just there. Subtle sounds may have previously gone unnoticed. Can you hear them now?

- **Touch** – Notice the feeling of your body in the chair. Notice the sensation of each part of your body in contact with the chair, becoming aware of how the chair holds your weight unconditionally. Notice the pressure between your feet and the floor. Notice the feeling of your hands on your lap, how the fabric of your clothes contacts your skin.

- **Breathing** – Now shift your concentration to your breathing. You're not trying to change your breathing – there is nothing to do right or wrong here, you're just noticing. Notice the sensations around your nose and mouth, as you gently breathe the cool air in. Notice the warm air as you exhale.

- **Thoughts** – If any thoughts come into your mind as you do this, just notice them, knowing there is nothing to do right, or to do wrong. Take a look at them, and maybe picture them as a phrase or image. Have a look at them for a moment, and when they're ready, let them drift away, like a stick on a stream. Once they have drifted away, bring your attention back to your breathing.

Once you have finished, bring your awareness to any noises around you, then take your own time to open your eyes.

Ask yourself these questions.

- What was happening in your body? Did you feel tense, or did you feel relaxed?
- Did you notice any emotions? Did you feel content and soothed, or anxious or have any mild feelings of low mood? What caused this?
- What was going through your mind? Did any thoughts come to mind? What were they? What did they look like?
- Did you notice things that you hadn't noticed before: sounds, physical sensations, thoughts or emotions?
- How might you use this new awareness in your work? Could you practise this before tasks or situations you find difficult? What do you want to become more aware of?
- How could you use that awareness to develop your skills and wellbeing?

Assessment

 Think

Most organisations offer the opportunity to complete a development assessment. In order to establish if this is right for you, consider the following questions.

- Who will carry out the assessment? What qualifications and experience do they have? Do you trust him or her? Will they bring out the best in you? Are they the sort of person you want to work with?

- What do you want the session to involve? Are there any topics you want to explore? What don't you want to cover? To what extent should it be forward or backward looking? Are there any particular psychometric assessments you would like included?

- Is it important to you to have a report based on the development assessment? What other outputs do you want? Do you want a personal development plan? How will you use this information?

- What are the boundaries in terms of confidentiality? Who will see the outputs? Who will hear about the session? What is the shelf-life of any reports produced? How will the information be used?

- Who will be funding the session? How much will it cost? Is there budget for this? What is the return on investment for you and the business?

- How long will the session take? Is there any pre-work? What needs to happen after the one to one? Do you have the time available to get the best out of the process for you and your business?

Notice Your Pattern of Response to Pressure

 Do

The thoughts, feelings and behaviours we engage in are like a steadily flowing stream. As they continuously flow, we can forget how we felt, thought and behaved quite quickly after an event, especially when we are under pressure. Take some time to think about what makes you stressed at work and explore this using the ABCD approach from Cognitive Behavioural Therapy. Keep a diary using the table below:

Activator (trigger)	Belief (thoughts)	Consequence (feelings, behaviours)
What made you feel pressured, stressed, anxious or low? Who was there? What happened? What were you doing at the time?	What did you think about yourself at the time? What did you think about the situation? What did you think about the other people involved? How strongly do you hold all of these beliefs (0–100%)?	How did you behave? How did you feel? What did other people do? What was the outcome? What impact did it have on your reputation at work? How did it change your performance? How did it make you feel about yourself?

Through this kind of monitoring of your experiences, you can begin to **look for patterns**. These patterns will be crucial in telling you about the kinds of responses you tend to have to pressure and stress. This will enable you to **dispute** any unhelpful beliefs and start reframing. You can then begin to think about the following questions:

- If you held a different belief about yourself in this situation, what might the effect be?
- What else could you have thought in that situation? Was there a more helpful way to think about that situation?
- Did you jump to conclusions? Did you guess what other people were thinking? Were you harsher on yourself than you would be on other people?
- Could you relate to your thoughts differently through mindfully recognising them, and 'letting them go' when they are ready to drift away? Consider the mindfulness techniques we looked at previously.
- When could you use these mindfulness techniques? Remember: thoughts are just thoughts, not facts!
- How else could you have behaved? What new ways of responding to that pressure or stress might have been helpful?
- What have you tried before when things have gone well?
- Who could help you to do that? What support do you need to do that?
- What else do you need to do to make that possible?

 Do

There are a number of online psychometric questionnaires designed to assess your reaction to pressure. For more information see **www.sane.works**

Consider Your Derailers

 Think

Have you ever derailed or felt yourself heading in that direction? Think of a time when you came off the rails or nearly came off the rails.

- What was the trigger?
- What impact did it have on your:
  - ◊ Mood?
  - ◊ Personality?
  - ◊ Style of relating to others?
  - ◊ Wellbeing?
  - ◊ Energy levels?
- What action did you take?
- What was the outcome?
- What feedback did you receive?
- What did you learn?
- What would you do differently next time?
- Is it true that you could overdo your strengths?

What are your **early warning signals** for next time you run this risk? How could you prevent it from happening?

 Do

There are a number of online questionnaires designed to measure your potential derailers. Our favourite is the Hogan Development Survey or HDS. For more information see **www.sane.works**

Notice Your OK-if Thoughts or Feelings

 Think

To try and bring your own rules for living to mind, consider the following questions.

1. What is important to you as a professional?
2. What skills or abilities do you pride yourself on?
3. What do you feel you do well?
4. What are you afraid you won't get right?
5. What do you feel you don't do well?
6. If you didn't do those things well, what would that mean for you?
7. What would that say about you?
8. What's the worst thing about that?
9. If you were to put that in an 'if I do X ... then I am Y' statement, what would that statement be?
10. How would it make you feel if you broke that 'if...then' statement?
11. Rate each rule from 0–10 (0 being no negative feelings at all, and 10 being the worst negative feelings you can imagine).

Once you have identified your rule(s) for living, it can be helpful to compare them. Rank them in order. Often, the one rated with the highest number can be the one which will cause you the most emotional pain if you break it. Therefore, it is possible that this rule also has a great effect on your behaviour, perhaps without you realising it.

If you have found a possible rule(s) for living, ask yourself these questions.

1. How likely is it that you may break this rule at some point?
2. What would the effect of this be on your self-esteem?
3. What would the effect be on how you think about yourself?
4. What would the impact of these consequences be on your functioning and performance in your professional role day to day?

Try and think of some easier rules to keep. These might be a little bit more flexible (such as, if I manage to do X some of the time, then I am Y), and/or recognise the limits of what you can do in the real world in a way that is fairer to you (for example, if I do X and it was in my control, then I might be Y).

Consider carrying around these statements on a post-it, or in a small journal, as reminders to you when you encounter situations that challenge your rules for living. They can be helpful reminders to be kinder and more understanding towards yourself, thereby helping you to reduce your risk of burn out.

 ## See

To gain a greater insight into your own personal rules for living, visit Sixth Sense Consulting Ltd. (www.sixthsenseconsulting.co.uk) to explore the range of assessment, coaching and psychotherapy services we can provide.

Larkin, P., (2014). *Collected Poems*. Faber and Faber.

Harris, T., (1967). *I'm OK, You're OK*. Arrow Books.

Lapworth, P. & Sills, C., (2011). *An Introduction to Transactional Analysis*. Sage.

Stewart, I. & Joines, V., (1987). *TA Today*. Lifespace Publishing.

What Are Your Drivers?

 Think

Reflect on the following questions in order to explore your drivers.

Do you feel you have a 'Be perfect' driver? In other words, you get rewarded (and feel OK) for getting things done right. If so:

- Both quality and quantity are important in most roles. Which is more important to you? Why?
- When have you had to compromise on quality? How did you feel? What was the worst thing that could have happened? Was the outcome as bad as you feared?
- Are there times when you haven't done something perfectly, but it's been valued by other people?
- How important is it to you to get something right first time? What reaction do you have when you have made a mistake? Was that as bad as you first thought? What does that tell you?

Do you have a 'Hurry up' driver? In other words, you get rewarded (and feel OK) for finishing things quickly. If so:

- How do you feel when you are faced with time delays that are beyond your control? What impact does it have on your behaviour?
- Think about a time when you wanted another person or group to 'hurry up'. How did you feel? What verbal and non-verbal cues did you give the other person (such as, glancing at your watch, fidgeting and interrupting)?

Do you have a 'Please others' driver? In other words, you have to get it right by others. If so:

- How do you feel if another person(s) is displeased with you? What happens if you feel you are being criticised or blamed?
- How do you respond when there is conflict or anger at work? How does it make you feel? How do you react?

- Think about a time when your goal was not aligned with the team's objectives. What did you do? Are there instances when you've disagreed with others and they've respected you?
- What might be some of the disadvantages of trying to please others? Do you get your own needs met – professional and/or personal – when you please other people? What emotions and thoughts come up if your needs aren't met?

Do you have a 'Try hard' driver? In other words, you must try hard (not necessarily to get a result) and it is the effort that counts. If so:

- How do you feel if you have tried hard but not finished something off? Do you sometimes give yourself 'points for trying', when you don't really intend to complete something?
- Do you get bored easily?
- How do you measure your success? Do you feel rebellious and non-compliant when you know there's no real point? Do you feel like kicking against the world and simply not playing ball?

Do you have a 'Be strong' driver? In other words, showing any sign of weakness means you are not OK. If so:

- How do you feel when a weakness is exposed? What's it like for you when you feel vulnerable?
- To what extent are you self-critical?
- If you were more compassionate towards yourself, what would that look like? What would you be thinking? What would you be doing?
- To what extent do you work long hours? What holds you back from delegating tasks? When do you ask for help?

 See

Joines, V. & Stewart, I., (2002). *Personality Adaptations*. Lifespace Publishing.

Do

There are a number of online questionnaires designed to measure your drivers. For more information see **www.sane.works**

Reflect on What Growing Up Was Like for You

 Do

Consider drawing out a timeline on a piece of paper. On the far left, write the date of your birth, and on the far right have the current date. Go through your life year by year, or decade by decade, and think of some of the key events and relationships throughout your life as you make your way along the line. Many people find these themes recur:

- Family relationships.
- Friendships.
- Intimate relationships.
- Experiences of being parented, and acting as a parent.
- School experiences (relationships with peers, teachers and figures of authority).
- Working life experiences (promotions, difficult events, redundancies, relationships with colleagues and superiors).
- Ill health (mental and physical).
- Substantial transitions (moving school, moving house, moving countries).
- Births.
- Deaths and losses.
- Key successes and failures.

This is not an exhaustive list, and you may find that you add to it and come up with events that don't fit into the categories above. The main thing is to highlight the key events for you.

A general rule is that, whilst all of your experiences are important, those that have the greatest impact on you tend to happen earlier, from your birth to late adolescence. Another general rule is that if similar kinds of events are experienced repeatedly, they will have a greater effect on how you see the world, yourself and other people than a single, stand-alone event. However, single events, if substantial enough in terms of their emotional and psychological significance, can have a notable impact too.

To get a greater sense of these, it may be worth talking with friends and family about your early life, to try and get multiple perspectives. It may be that other people remember things you don't, and can help piece together a richer, more detailed description of your life history.

 Think

Ask yourself these questions.

- What has shaped you as a person?
- Who was a role model for you in early life?
- What are some of your earliest memories?
- Can you recall some of your favourite stories relating to your childhood?
- How were you parented?
- How did your mum/dad show approval?
- How did they show disapproval?
- How were you rewarded?
- How were you punished?
- What sayings did your mum or dad have about life?
- What advice did they give you about life in general?
- How did your parents describe success in life?
- What feelings, thoughts or beliefs were encouraged in you?
- What feelings, thoughts or beliefs were discouraged or prohibited?

- What did your mum/dad want you to be?
- What was your childhood home(s) like?
- How would you describe the area you grew up in?

 See

Branch, R. & Wilson, R., (2010). *Cognitive Behavioural Therapy for Dummies*. John Wiley & Sons.

Despite the name, this is a good introduction to CBT theory, and includes information about rules for living, core beliefs and aspects of interpersonal styles. It clearly sets out how early experiences impact our day-to-day living.

Think About How the Scarf Model Applies to You

 Do

During this activity, consider your needs in the areas of Status, Certainty, Autonomy, Relatedness and Fairness. Ask yourself the following questions to help with this activity.

Status

- What does the word 'status' mean to you?
- Which relationships matter to you most at work? Why are they important?
- Have you felt inferior in those relationships compared to another person/other people? Who was that? How did it make you feel?
- When was the most recent time that you felt inferior? What did the other person/people do to trigger that?
- What did you think in that situation? What feelings came up for you (for example, anger, sadness)?
- What did you actually do in that situation? How did it affect your behaviour?
- When have you recently felt that you had greater status?
- Who was there? What did they do?
- What affect did that have on how you felt about yourself and your situation at the time?
- How did that affect your behaviour at the time with other people?
- How has that affected your behaviour since with other people?
- Has that helped or hindered your ability to have healthy relationships with others?

- How important is it to you to enhance your status at work?
- What would greater status look like? What would it feel like?
- What role would you have? What would you be doing? How would other people be behaving towards you?
- What can you do to improve your sense of status? Could you improve your sense of status by learning something new, or developing yourself in some way? What would that be?

Certainty

- What does the word certainty mean to you?
- What do you have certainty about at work?
- When was the last time you felt uncertain or anxious about your future at work?
- What happened before and during that time to create that uncertainty?
- How did you feel at that time?
- What were you thinking at that time of uncertainty?
- How did that impact on your behaviour? How did you behave differently towards other people?
- Was that helpful or unhelpful? What told you it was helpful/unhelpful?
- What would have helped in that situation to increase your sense of certainty? Who could have played a part in that?
- What could you do to increase your feelings of certainty? What would that look like? What would you be doing? What would you be feeling like?
- Who could help you to achieve that?

Autonomy

- What does the word autonomy mean to you?
- When have you felt you had greater control over your behaviour?

- What was going on at the time? What happened?
- What did you do to facilitate that? What did other people do to facilitate that?
- What told you that you had greater control? Consider your thoughts, feelings and behaviour at the time.
- When have you felt out of control at work in relation to your own behaviour, beliefs or environment?
- What happened to trigger that?
- How did you feel (for example, angry, sad)?
- What did you think at the time about yourself? About other people?
- How did that impact your behaviour with other people?
- Was that helpful or unhelpful? What told you that it was helpful/ unhelpful?
- What would greater autonomy look like? What would you be doing differently in terms of your behaviour, emotional state and thoughts?

Relatedness

- What does the word relatedness mean to you?
- Think about key relationships at work. How would you classify them? Are they: trusting or untrusting, safe or threatening, consistent or unreliable?
- Do you notice that particular choices are more common than others?
- How does that pattern affect how you feel around people in your role day to day? For example, do you feel anxious or relaxed when around other people?
- How does that affect your behaviour? For example, do you turn to others for support, or do you shut them out and try to avoid them?

- What other impact does that have on your behaviour day to day? For example, do you work with others on new opportunities? Do you often play it safe when working with others and 'keep your head down'?

Fairness

- What does fairness mean to you in the workplace?
- What would fairness look like? What would other people be doing? What would you be doing?
- What tells you that something is fair or not fair? What feelings come up that tell you that?
- When was the last time that something unfair happened at work?
- Who was involved? What happened that was unfair?
- What about that was unfair?
- What feelings came up for you at that time?
- How did that affect your behaviour with other people?
- What was the outcome of that?
- What did you learn from that?
- What did other people say about your actions?
- What could you do in future to improve fairness in your role?

 See

Brehm, J.W., (1966). *A Theory of Psychological Reactance*. New York: Academic Press.

Brehm, S.S. & Brehm, J.W., (1981). *Psychological Reactance: A Theory of Freedom and Control*. New York: Academic Press.

Maslow, A. H., (1943). A theory of human motivation. *Psychological Review*, 50, pp. 370–396.

Miller, W. R. & Rollnick, S., (2002). *Motivational Interviewing: Preparing People for Change* (2nd edition). Guilford Press: London.

Rock, D., (2008). SCARF: A brain-based model for collaborating with and influencing others. *NeuroLeadership Journal*, 1, pp. 1–9.

Rock, D., (2009). *Your Brain at Work: Strategies for Overcoming Distraction, Regaining Focus, and Working Smarter All Day Long*. Harper Business.

Learn About Transactional Analysis (TA)

 Do

The best way to learn about transactional analysis is to do some reading and to book onto a TA101 course. Simply search for TA101 in your area and see what comes up. Make sure that the course tutor is fully qualified (they should have the designation TSTA) and provides an official certificate at the end. These courses are usually two days and many of them run over a weekend. The governing body for TA in Europe is EATA (European Association of Transactional Analysis) and outside the UK it's the ITAA (International Transactional Analysis Association), so you can always check course providers out this way.

 See

Lapworth, P. & Sills, C., (2011). *An Introduction to Transactional Analysis*. Sage.

Mountain, A. & Davidson, C., (2011). *Working Together*. Gower.

Stewart, I. & Joines, V., (1987). *TA Today*. Lifespace Publishing.

Try the PAC model

 Do

Next time you are having a conversation with someone at work, consider the ego state that you are both in and pay attention to the pattern of your conversation.

Paying attention to feelings is one way. Do you feel like scolding the other person or perhaps looking after them? If this is the case, you could be in a Parent ego state and your transactions with the other person could be stimulating them to respond as a Child. It could also be the other way around. If you feel vulnerable, young or you feel like being looked after, you are probably in a Child ego state and thereby inviting the other person to behave as a Parent towards you. If you are both having a 'grown-up conversation', dealing with the issue at hand in a calm and rational way, then you are having an adult-to-adult transaction.

Another way is to look at behaviour.

- **Parent** – Look for tense body language: arms folded, clenched fists, tight jaw, sharp voice, falling inflexion, words like 'should', 'must', 'have to' and a narrative of one-up.
- **Adult** – Look for balanced and well-grounded sitting or standing positions, relaxed posture, deep and regular breathing, clarity of thought, even-tempo inflexion in speech and an open, non-judgemental narrative.
- **Child** – Look for dropped shoulders, bowed head, muttering, avoidance of eye contact, agitated body language, rising inflexion (this one is less reliable these days as it's becoming a universal habit!) and a narrative which talks of needing permission, approval or sounds unreasonably rebellious.

If you are adopting an ego state other than Adult, try changing your response style and see what happens.

Reflect on Your Attachment Patterns

 Think

Reflect on the following questions.

Personal life

- Do you want to be emotionally close to someone?
- What characteristics do you look for when building a deeper relationship with somebody?
- What do you find hard about being emotionally close to someone (if anything)?
- Think of one person you are close to outside of work?
    - ◊ What do you like about that relationship?
    - ◊ What are you afraid might happen in that relationship?
    - ◊ What would you like to change in the relationship?
    - ◊ How would you feel if you no longer had a relationship with that person?
    - ◊ What do you think that tells you about what you want in relationships?
    - ◊ What does that tell you about your attachment style?
    - ◊ What is helpful about that? What is unhelpful?
    - ◊ What would you want to change?

Professional Life

- Who do you feel close to at work (if anyone)?
- If you aren't close to anyone, what stops you from doing that?
- How do you feel about building a relationship with new business contacts?
- What first impression do you think you create?
- What feedback have you had (if any) about your relationship building skills?

- How could you gain that feedback?
- What has your reaction been, or what would your reaction be if you received critical feedback?
- What has that done/what would that do to your relationship with that person?
- Do you think that is helpful/would be helpful to you, and to others in work?
- What do you/would you want to change about that?

See

Bowlby, J., (2005). *The Making and Breaking of Affectional Bonds.* Oxon: Routledge Classics.

De Botton, A., (2004). *Status Anxiety.* Penguin

Fox, K., (2004). *Watching the English.* Hodder & Stoughton

Sable, P., (2007). What is adult attachment? *Clinical Social Work Journal*, 36, pp. 21–30.

Safran, J. D., (1990a). Towards a refinement of cognitive therapy in light of interpersonal theory: I. Theory. *Clinical Psychology Review*, 10, pp. 87–105.

Safran, J. D., (1990b). Towards a refinement of cognitive therapy in light of interpersonal theory: II. Practice. *Clinical Psychology Review*, 10, pp. 107–121.

Safran, J. D. & Segal, Z. V., (1990). *Interpersonal Process in Cognitive Therapy.* New York: Basic Books.

Think About a Relationship that Feels Stuck or Difficult

 Do

If you find yourself in a difficult or stuck relationship, try the following activity as a way of considering where the problem lies, and what you may be able to do to start fixing it.

Step One – Psychological Awareness

- Which relationship(s) feels difficult or stuck? Who is that person(s) and how do you know them?

- When was the last time the relationship felt stuck? What was the situation (where were you, what were you doing at the time)? Be specific.

- What did the other person do to make the relationship feel difficult or stuck? What did you do to make the relationship feel difficult or stuck? Be specific.

- What feelings did that bring up for you? Summarise that in a statement, such as 'I felt X'.

- Try and recall the type of event, or better yet a specific example of when the person(s) made you last feel that way. Recalling a recent example will be easier than recalling a more distant one.

- Include that event in the 'I felt X' statement, as such that you might now say 'I felt X, when you did Y'.

- What would you have liked the person to have done instead? Try and highlight what you felt you needed from them. What would have been so good about that? What would that have indicated about you?

- Write down what you needed from them and why that would have been helpful for you. Include that in the 'I felt X, when you did Y' statement. It should now read something like 'I felt X, when you did Y, and I would like you to do a different Y in future as that would give me Z'.

Once you have done this, proceed to step two.

Step Two – Barriers to Communication

- Would you feel able to communicate this 'I' statement to the person(s) who makes you feel this way?
- If not, what would be the worst thing about saying this to that person(s)? What would be the worst thing that could happen? Is this a realistic prediction?
- What would make it easier to say what you want to say? Could you consider other settings which may make it easier: individually as opposed to a group setting? In an informal setting (such as lunch or after work) rather than in a formal setting (as in a meeting or group task)?
- Consider whether another medium of communication would be helpful – would it be easier on the telephone or via letter rather than face to face? Consider that face-to-face communication is often much clearer than emails, texts or other indirect means of communication.
- Remember that there is a big difference between assertiveness and aggression or rudeness. The former views your own opinion and those of other people as having equal right and status, the latter views your opinion as more important than others'.
- It is OK to be assertive. In fact it helps maintain psychological health and wellbeing.

If you feel able to communicate your 'I' statement to the person(s) you have in mind, proceed to step three.

Step Three – Communicating Your Needs

- Before you speak to the person(s) you want to speak to, check that you have been through steps 1 and 2, and have an idea of what your 'I' statement will be.
- Anxiety can impact on your ability to think clearly. Try and relax. Be aware of any unhelpful thoughts and emotions, and let them go.

- When you speak to the person, firstly provide a brief introduction to what you are going to say next (i.e. your 'I' statement). This will help to provide an informal agenda of what you will discuss, and will prepare the person for what is coming next. This might be something like 'Thanks for agreeing to talk with me, I was hoping we could discuss something that I've been thinking about and that's concerning me'.
- State your 'I' statement. Take your time, be assertive.
- Once you've provided your 'I' statement, make sure the person understands. To do this, ask questions such as 'What do you understand from what I've said'? Clarify any misinterpretations they've made. It can be helpful to use the same style of language they use, as that will make it easier for them to understand.
- Invite their views and be willing to negotiate. It is important to recognise, respect and try to get your needs met; however, it might be that you need to compromise with the person about how to do that. Be prepared to be flexible, and listen to the other person.
- Above all, try to be honest about your thoughts, feelings and needs.

 See

American Psychiatric Association. (2014) *Diagnostic and Statistical Manual of Mental Disorders* – Fifth Edition (DSM-5).

Babiak, D., & Hare, R., (2006). *Snakes in Suits*. Harper.

Berne, E., (1964). *Games People Play*. Grove Press.

Briers, S., (2012). *Brilliant Cognitive Behavioural Therapy: How to Use CBT to Improve Your Mind and Your Life*. Pearson.

Brown, J., (1997). Circular Questioning: An introductory guide. *Australian & New Zealand Journal of Family Therapy*, 18, pp. 109–114. Good introduction to the idea of how people can mutually influence each other in relationships to cause relationship difficulties.

Dutton, K., (2012). *The Wisdom of Psychopaths.* Heinemann

James, O., (2013). *Office Politics.* Vermilion.

Karpman, S., (1967, 2007). USATAA/ITAA conference lecture August 11, 2007, free download at http://www.karpmandramatriangle.com/pdf/thenewdramatriangles.pdf

Maslow, A. H., (1943). A theory of human motivation. *Psychological Review,* 50, pp. 370–396. Classic text on the concept of human needs and how they drive motivation.

McGrath, H. & Edwards, H., (2009). *Difficult Personalities.* Penguin.

Rollnick, S., Miller, W. R. & Butler, C. C. (2008). *Motivational Interviewing in Health Care.* New York: Guilford Press.

Stone, L., See www.lindastone.net for a wealth of resources on continuous partial attention.

Westbrook, D., Kennerley, H. & Kirk, J., (2007). *An Introduction to CBT: Skills and Applications.* Sage Publications. A good brief introduction to CBT concepts.

Try Satir's Daily Temperature Reading

 Do

Try this questionnaire. Be as honest as you can in answering the questions, and reflect on what you would like to do in the future given the answers you've provided.

- Think about a relationship that really matters to you at work.
- List as many things as possible that you really appreciate about this person. Try to name values or characteristics this person holds which you appreciate (for example, they may be trustworthy, caring, committed).
- Which of these have you told the other person about?
- Which of these haven't you told the other person?

- What is it that prevents you from saying this to the other person?
- How would you feel if someone said that to you?
- What would have to happen for you to tell the other person?
- What values do you hold which are important in your work life?
- What hopes and dreams do you have at work that are perhaps based on these values?
- Where do you hope to be in five years' time at work? What will you be doing, where will you be, what role will you hold? Be specific.
- Does the other person know about these values, hopes and dreams?
- What can you do to help them learn about your values and hopes?
- What puzzles you about your relationship with this person?
- What are you curious about?
- What causes you to feel uneasy in this relationship?
- What would have to happen for you to tell this person about your curiosities and what you feel uneasy about? What can you do to facilitate that happening?
- What needs do you have that aren't being met in this relationship (such as, self-worth, feeling cared for, acknowledgement of your career ambitions)?
- What would tell you that these needs had been met? What would that look like? How would you be behaving, feeling, thinking? How would the other person be behaving?
- Does this person know about these needs?
- What can the other person do to help meet these needs?
- What could you do to let them know that?

 See

Satir, V., (1991). *Virginia Satir: Foundational Ideas*. Binghamton: Taylor & Francis Inc.

Notice How You Tend to Filter Incoming Information

 Do

To begin with it's important to work out whether there are any filters that may be unhelpful for you on a day-to-day basis. Try the activity below and answer the questions as honestly as you can. If you believe that unhelpful filters are present, consider moving on to the next step.

Step One – Detecting Filters

- Do you feel that you have unhelpful beliefs about yourself, your future, other people or the world around you? What are these beliefs? Try writing them down on a piece of paper and be specific.

- If you wrote down more than one belief, ask yourself which one brings up the most unhelpful emotions for you? Rate them from 0–10, 10 being the most emotion you could possibly feel from that belief, and 0 being none at all. Rank those beliefs on the basis of that rating in order, from highest to lowest.

- Look at the list and consider which one may be easiest to focus on first; it may not be the one that arouses the most emotion for you.

- Thinking about that belief, when was the last time that you thought that? Think about the event. What was going on around you? What did you do? Who was there? What happened? Again, be as specific as you can.

- What information told you that that belief was true? Do you often notice information like that?

- Try keeping a diary for a week or two. Write down each time an unhelpful thought or belief comes to mind. Note down what tells you that belief or thought is true each time. Try to do it in the moment, as it's often hard to recall thoughts and information after the event has passed.

- Look at the diary at the end of the week. Do you notice anything about the information you've written down? Are there any themes to the information you've been noticing? What are you paying most attention to? What are you filtering out or paying little attention to?

- Ask yourself whether that information reflects all the facts of what you've experienced over the past week or two? What is the impact of noticing that kind of information on your emotions? What is helpful about it?

- Try repeating this process for other unhelpful beliefs, working your way up the list to beliefs that are perhaps more difficult to think about.

If after this process you feel that you may benefit from some strategies to manage the impact of your filters, consider the next steps.

Step Two – Strategies to Manage Your Filters

- Try using the mindfulness exercises in Chapter 4 and the YouTube links to mindfulness exercises available on **www.sane.works** to begin to notice when your filters are affecting you, and to let go of any unhelpful predictions or emotions that may impact your performance.

- Try using relaxation strategies such as progressive muscular relaxation to reduce your physical anxiety levels. There are lots of useful apps that can help you with this. You could start with Andrew Johnson's Relax+. Something like this will help to reduce any physical anxiety which might impact on your performance day to day.

- Use the thought-challenging diary below to write down your thoughts about the situation and to consider alternative thoughts which may be fairer to you and more helpful.

- Try a mindfulness meditation.

- Try a positive data diary or log. Consider the beliefs you high-lighted in Step One. What information might tell you that wasn't true? What would that look like? What would you be doing? What would other people be doing? Keep a diary or pad with you and write down each time you notice something, no matter how small, that tells you that belief isn't true. For example, if you were to have the belief that 'I'm a failure at work', information which may dispute that belief could include a time when some-one has complimented you on previous work, a time when you helped a colleague with advice, or favourable feedback during a meeting. These are just some examples, so it's important to take some time to really think what kinds of things, large and small, may tell you your belief isn't true. Be wary of discounting positive information as 'exceptions that prove the rule'; this might be a sign of your filter. Try keeping this diary or pad for several weeks, and write the information down immediately after the event to make sure you remember it. At the end of this period, review your pad or diary and reflect on what this information tells you about your belief.

Step Three – Review Your Progress

After you have tried some of the strategies above, reflect on their out-come. Did they help? What told you that they were helpful? What could you do to make sure you keep using those strategies?

If they weren't helpful, then that's sometimes to be expected. It can be the case that some strategies that work for some people don't work for others. Try experimenting with some of the other strategies mentioned above and see whether they work for you. Ask yourself the questions in the paragraph above to evaluate whether they have been helpful.

If they haven't, consider whether you may need some additional sup-port in the form of coaching or psychotherapy to consider your filters and their impact, and to work out how you may be able to work to-gether with a professional to manage and change those filters over time. Chapter 5 of this book talks about how you could choose someone to help you.

 See

If you would like to explore coaching, please visit Sixth Sense Consulting Ltd. (www.sixthsenseconsulting.co.uk), which provides a range of assessment, coaching and psychotherapy services for business.

 See

Batten, S. J., (2011). *Essentials of Acceptance and Commitment Therapy*. Sage: London.

Fennell, M. J. V., (2009). *Overcoming Low Self-Esteem: A Self-Help Guide Using Cognitive Behavioural Techniques*. Robinson.

Harris, R., (2009). *ACT Made Simple: A Quick-Start Guide to ACT Basics and Beyond*. Oakland, CA: New Harbinger Publications Inc.

Deconstruct a Difficult Day

 Do

Many strategies have been discussed so far, which can be helpful in managing the impact of challenging events and the thoughts and emotions they can produce. Another potentially useful strategy taken from CBT is that of challenging unhelpful thoughts by considering whether they are illogical or relatively unfounded. To do this, it can be useful to use a 'thought diary', such as the example on pages 246–247.

This thought diary is similar to the one we talked about in relation to you under pressure in that it asks you to document times when you have experienced an unhelpful thought, the trigger(s) for it, the thought itself and its consequences.

However, this approach goes one step further. It also asks you to consider whether there are any examples of thought errors. For example, someone who thinks 'I'll never get a promotion' after a 360° feedback session which involved some critiques, may notice that they are engaging in over-generalisation and negative filtering.

Each time you notice a negative thought, write down the information in each of the columns, including information about any thought errors you notice. Once you have done that, review the thought itself and thought errors column and consider what a fairer, more accurate and helpful thought may be, given any thought errors you've noticed. We're not looking to replace the unhelpful thought with one that is unrealistically positive or optimistic; just one that is fairer to you and more helpful, given all the information you have. Consider from 0–100% how much you believe that thought.

Often when people first begin using this strategy, they may notice that the extent to which they believe the alternative thought is less than they believe their original unhelpful thought. This is not uncommon, and is often a reflection of the fact that unhelpful thinking has taken root over time, and has become automatic. It can take time and practice for the new, fairer and more helpful thoughts to take root and to 'feel' real, as they gradually begin to replace the automatic unhelpful thoughts.

Like any new skill, this takes practice. As such, it is advised that you practise this new strategy each time an unhelpful thought arises. Obviously, this will depend on practicalities, but it is important to try to engage with thought challenging whenever possible because the natural urge can sometimes be to avoid this type of activity, as it requires people to look at what can be very upsetting thoughts. This is natural, and is an understandable response to what can be an unpleasant experience to begin with.

Activator (trigger) What happened? Who was there? What were you doing at the time?	Belief (thoughts) What did you think at the time? How much did you believe that (0–100%)?	Consequence (feelings, behaviours) How did you behave? How did you feel?

Thought error	Alternative thought
What errors in your thinking did you notice? (See Chapter 4 for more information about the types of thought errors people can experience.)	Given any errors in your thinking, what might be an alternative thought? How much do you believe that thought (0–100%)?

However, avoiding the issue is unhelpful as it doesn't actually resolve the problem. Practising thought challenging when you can offers a longer-term strategy to deal with unhelpful thinking, and the sooner and more often you practise it, the more you will improve and the sooner you will potentially benefit from its use. Also, try to use this strategy in the moment – when the unhelpful thought happens – as thoughts are often fleeting and it can be hard to remember and challenge unhelpful thoughts after they have passed (which they invariably do).

 ## See

Beck, A. T., (1976). *Cognitive Therapy and the Emotional Disorders*. International Universities Press.

Beck, A. T., Greenberger, D. & Padesky, C. A., (1995). *Mind Over Mood: Change How You Feel by Changing the Way You Think*. Guilford Press.

Burns, D. D., (1999). *The Feeling Good Handbook*. New York, NY: Plume.

Drapeau, M. & Perry, C. J., (2010). *Cognitive Errors Rating Scales* (3rd Ed.). McGill Group.

Joseph, A. & Chapman, M., (2013). *Visual CBT*. Capstone.

Layard, R., (2005). *Happiness: Lessons from a New Science*. Penguin.

Nelson, P., (1993). *There's a Hole in My Sidewalk: The Romance of Self-Discovery*. Beyond Words Publishing Inc.

Peters, S., (2011). *The Chimp Paradox*. Vermilion.

Ricard, M., (2003). *Happiness*. Altantic Books.

Ricard, M., (2008). *The Art of Meditation*. Atlantic Books.

Sacco, W.P. & Beck, A.T., (1995). Cognitive Theory and Therapy. In E. Edward Beckham and William R. Leber (Eds.), *Handbook of Depression: Treatment, Assessment and Research* (2nd ed.). New York: Guilford Press.

Tolle, E., (1999). *The Power of Now*. New World Library

Tolle, E., (2005). *A New Earth*. Penguin

Westbrook, D., Kennerley, H. & Kirk, J., (2007). *An Introduction to Cognitive Behaviour Therapy: Skills and Applications*. Sage.

Reflect on Passivity

 Think

You might consider being passive as doing nothing, which it can be. But it can also be a number of other non-problem-solving behaviours. Think about a problem where you feel stuck and unhappy. Are you doing any of the following?

- **Doing nothing** – This can actually be OK if you are making a conscious decision to do nothing at this point because that's best. If you are feeling cool, calm and collected and choosing not to take action, that's one thing; but if you are doing nothing because you are frozen with fear and as immobile as a rabbit in headlights, that's quite another.

- **Over-adapting** – This is where you are not pursuing your goal but you are working to achieve someone else's when it's not in your interest to do so. Over-adapting is frequently a feature of unbalanced or abusive relationships.

- **Agitating** – This is an angry, worried or anxious response to a problem where you try over and over again to arrive at a solution using the same repertoire of behaviours. Imagine you have lost your mobile phone and you keep looking in the same place, over and over again!

- **Incapacitation** – This is where instead of staying with the problem, you retreat to a sanctuary of illness or intoxication. You 'lose it' or you hit the bottle. The problem, of course, doesn't go away.

- **Violence** – This is not necessarily connected with hitting people or kicking the cat; inanimate objects will do. Smashing up your office will not take you any closer to a solution to a workplace problem!

 See

Schiff, A. & Schiff, J., Passivity. *Transactional Analysis Journal*. January 1971; vol. 1, 1: pp. 71–78.

Practise Mindfulness and Learn to Meditate

 Do

Book onto a short course on mindfulness meditation. There are plenty to choose from. For example, in London, there's the excellent School of Life (www.theschooloflife.com) and in Manchester, there's Breathworks (www.breathworks-mindfulness.org.uk).

 See

Halliwell, E. & Heaversedge, J., (2012). *The Mindful Manifesto: How Doing Less and Noticing More Can Help Us Thrive in a Stressed-Out World*. Hay House.

Kabat-Zin, J., (2004). *Wherever You Go, There You Are: Mindfulness Meditation in Everyday Life*. Piatkus.

Maharaj, S., (2012). *I Am That: Talks With Sri Nisargadatta Maharaj*. Acorn Press.

Nelson, P., (2012). *There's a Hole in My Sidewalk: The Romance of Self-Discovery*. Beyond Words Publishing.

Williams, M. & Penman, D., (2011). *Mindfulness: A Practical Guide to Finding Peace in a Frantic World*. Piatkus.

The World Happiness Report 2013 can be downloaded from: http://unsdsn.org/resources/publications/world-happiness-report-2013/

Explore Your Resilience

 Do

Access the *i-resilience* questionnaire at www.robertsoncooper.com/iresilience

 Think

Think of a current problem at work in the light of your *i-resilience* report and a problem that you have successfully tackled in the past.

- **Coping skills** – Was there a time in the past when you experienced a similar problem? How did you cope? What action did you take to manage the challenge?

- **Support networks** – What support networks did you use in the past when you experienced a problem? Were there different types of support you needed (such as, personal emotional support, professional support)? Who was good at providing particular kinds of support?

- **Religion, Faith and Values** – Did your religion, faith or personal values help? In what way?

- **Role models** – Who was an important role model for you then? In what way did they help you?

- **Problem-solving skills** – What problem-solving skills did you use in the past to help you manage problems?

- **Emotional support** – What emotional support did you draw upon in the past? How did you obtain it? Who helped you? What exactly did they do to help? Are particular people better at meeting particular needs? Is it better to speak to some people about practical work problems, and others about personal emotional difficulties?

- **Resourcefulness** – What other resources did you draw upon? What impact did this have?

- **Personal control** – How aware were you of your problems and their impact? When did you first notice this impact? What were the signs; emotionally, physically, socially? What steps did you take to manage the problems before they worsened?

- **Self-esteem** – How did you maintain self-esteem? What things did you take a sense of purpose from? What activities or roles did you see as important to you? Are those activities and other things important and helpful now? What new things can you do that you could take purpose from?

- **Self-talk** – When you think about past examples of how you managed difficulties or problems what useful things did you say to yourself that helped you?

- **Fitness** – What did you do to ensure you maintained an active lifestyle? How did you maintain your energy levels? What was the result? How did it make you feel?

- **Rest and relaxation** – When have you faced similar challenges in the past? What did you do to ensure you had sufficient rest and relaxation?

- **Bounce back** – What did you do to bounce back from setbacks? What did you learn from the experience?

 ## See

Jones, G., (2009). *Thriving on Pressure*. Easton Studio Press

Tugade, M., Fredrickson B. & Barrett, L., (2004). Psychological Resilience and Positive Emotional Granularity: Examining the benefits of positive emotions on coping and health. *Journal of Personality*, 72, pp. 1161–1190.

Webb, L., (2013). *Resilience*. Capstone

Healthy Body, Healthy Mind

 Think

There are various methods, treatments and therapies used in safe-guarding wellbeing, and the prevention or reduction of stress, for example:

- Yoga
- Reflexology
- Acupuncture
- Reiki
- Socially connecting with other people
- Volunteering
- Hypnotherapy
- Joy and laughter
- Fresh air and physical exercise
- Fun and games
- Hobbies and interests
- Diet and hydration
- Coaching, counselling, therapy

Can you think of any other approaches to look after your wellbeing? If so, add them to the list above.

Highlight the ones you have tried. Give them a rating of 1–10 in terms of how effective they are in maintaining your personal wellbeing. Which of these could you do more of? What is holding you back? How can you break down any barriers? What else are you open to trying on the list? What actions are you going to take to maximise your wellbeing?

 # Think

Think about your health.

- When did you last have a health check?
- What are your current health-related concerns, if any?
- What holds you back from addressing any concerns?
- What support do you need?
- What first step will you take?
- When will you do this?

 # Do

Keep a relaxation diary.

- Keep a record of any relaxation technique or activity you undertake.
- Note down the date and the time.
- What does being relaxed mean to you? What would it look like? What would you be thinking, doing, feeling in your body that would tell you that you were relaxed?
- Record how effective each technique or activity was by rating it on a scale of 1 to 10 (1 = not effective and 10 = highly effective).
- How could you get into the habit of relaxing more often?
- What places do you have which are quiet and comfortable, where you won't be disturbed by others?
- How would you go about creating that kind of space?

 Think

Consider the following questions if you're trying to determine whether you may benefit from coaching or therapy. Ask yourself:

- To what extent am I happy at work? Do I act and feel as though I am enjoying my role?
- Do I feel that I gain a sense of meaning, and that I am being challenged in my role at work?
- Am I experiencing a significant problem at work?
- What feedback have I received on my performance?
- Am I feeling frustrated or without direction or purpose in my career?
- Do I feel as though my thoughts, beliefs, behaviour or emotions are holding me back in the workplace? Am I getting stuck in the same old patterns of behaviour without progress?
- Do I feel comfortable or unhappy about these things? Would I benefit from changing some of these things?
- What have I tried to remedy this situation? How did that work out?
- What would I hope to gain from coaching that I couldn't do myself? In what ways would it benefit me?
- If I had coaching and I improved in the way I hoped, what would that look like in my 'mind's eye'?
- How would I be behaving differently, thinking differently, feeling differently if coaching was successful?
- What would have to happen in my career to tell me coaching had been worthwhile?

 See

Dexter, J., Dexter, G., & Irving, J., (2011). *An Introduction to Coaching*. London: Sage Publications.

Kline, N., (1999). *Time to Think*. Octopus Publishing

Star, J., (2008). *The Coaching Manual*. Pearson – Prentice Hall.

Prochaska, J. O., Norcross, J., & DiClemente, C. C., (1994). *Changing for Good*. Collins.

Whitmore, J., (1992). *Coaching for Performance*. Nicholas Brealey

Professional Bodies and Sources of Information

Organisation	Website
Association for Coaching (AC)	www.associationforcoaching.com
British Association for Counselling and Psychotherapy (BACP)	www.bacp.co.uk
British Psychological Society (BPS)	www.bps.org.uk
Coaching Directory	www.coach-search.co.uk
Counselling Directory	www.counselling-directory.org.uk
European Coaching and Mentoring Council (EMCC)	www.emccouncil.org/uk
International Coach Federation (ICF)	www.coachfederation.org.uk
United Kingdom Council for Psychotherapy (UKCP)	www.ukcp.org.uk

Index